CITIZENS OF TWO WORLDS

Religion and Politics among
American Seventh-day Adventists

•A15045 208448

CITIZENS OF TWO WORLDS

Religion and Politics among
American Seventh-day Adventists

BR
115
.P7
D78
1992
West

Roger L. Dudley and Edwin I. Hernandez

Andrews University Press   Berrien Springs, MI 49104

Copyright 1992
Andrews University Press
Berrien Springs, MI 49104

All rights reserved. No part of this publication may be reproduced, stored in a retrieval system, or transmitted in any form or by any means—electronic, mechanical, photocopying, recording, or otherwise—without the prior permission of the copyright owner.

ISBN 0-943872-66-9
Library of Congress Catalog Card Number 92-071514

Printing: 7 6 5 4 3 2 1   Year: 98 97 96 95 94 93 92

Printed by Patterson Printing Company
Benton Harbor, Michigan

Cover design by Ria Fisher, Spectradesign, Berrien Springs, MI

Cover color separations and imaging by LithoMark, Stevensville, MI

Dedicated

To our wives, Margaret (Peggy) Dudley and Maggie Hernandez, whose patient and loving support provided the encouragement we needed to complete this monumental task.

Table of Contents

Chapter 1	A Puzzling Relationship	1
Chapter 2	Made in America	19
Chapter 3	The Jewel of Consistency	41
Chapter 4	Adventism and Politics in Historical Perspective	59
Chapter 5	The Adventist Connection	81
Chapter 6	The Religion of American Adventists . . .	99
Chapter 7	Social Sources of Religious Commitment	127
Chapter 8	The Politics of American Adventists . . .	149
Chapter 9	How Religion Informs Political Positions	165
Chapter 10	Social Sources of Political Positions	191
Chapter 11	Making Sense out of It All	213
Chapter 12	Overcoming the Great Fallacy	233
Chapter 13	New Directions for the Church	277
APPENDIX:	Methodology of the Study	313

Chapter 1

A Puzzling Relationship

Modern Americans live in a society where they are encouraged and expected to participate in the political process. They vote for candidates and issues. They form and express opinions on various public questions. Sometimes they write position letters to media editors, and occasionally they join in rallies for or against some cause. They generally identify themselves with some sort of political ideology.

Contrasting Groups

One way to look at the question is to ask if differences exist among Catholics, Protestants, and Jews on public issues and voting patterns. Historically, Protestants have been more likely to vote Republican, and Catholics and Jews to vote Democrat. In fact, since 1952 the majority of Protestants have voted Republican in every presidential election except that of 1964.[1] As Johnstone reminds us, however, these differences cannot be traced totally and simply to religion since a relationship between religion and social class has been demonstrated to exist, and social class is known to influence political ideology. Also, changing societal conditions may be eroding the relationship, as citizens perceive it in their interest to switch traditional partisan allegiances.

Wald[2] presents a different grouping when he divides churches into evangelical and mainline with the former tending to be conservative in public affairs and the latter liberal. Even here, however, the distinction is not clear-cut for Wald shows how predominantly black churches combine the theological affinities associated with evangelicalism with the progressive social role championed by mainline Protestantism.

Roozen, McKinney, and Carroll in their attempt to relate religion to social attitudes have proposed two types of congregations, the this-worldly and the other-worldly. This-worldly parishes encourage their people to become deeply involved in ministry to social ills. Christians establish the kingdom of God as they work to bless society. Other-worldly parishes withdraw from a tarnished world and seek isolation for their people in a common ritual and prayer life. They seek to win individuals to their faith with the promise of salvation beyond this life.[3]

A fourth method of categorizing is the sect-denomination classification. Sects exist in high tension with contemporary society, have exclusive membership requirements, and tend to focus on other-worldly concerns. By contrast, denominations are more likely to accommodate to the culture, be more inclusive in membership, and be more occupied with temporal concerns.[4] Obviously, such differences affect attitudes toward public issues.

All of the above groupings assume that members within a given faith share the same religious experience, and, therefore, to the extent that religion influences public policy, they might be expected to have similar views on socio-political issues. While this may be true to some extent, a wide variety of religious beliefs and behaviors exists among the members of most denominations.[5] Thus it would be appropriate to attempt to determine how religious variation *within* a particular denomination affects attitudes toward public issues as well as to study how these attitudes vary *across* denominational lines. Such relationships have been explored within the Roman Catholic Church,[6] the Lutheran Church in America,[7] the Mennonite Church,[8] and the Reformed Church in America[9] among others.

This book is also concerned with a single denomination–the Seventh-day Adventist Church in the United States. While some historical accounts exist, very little if any field study has been conducted on the attitudes of Adventists toward public issues. The

Chapter 1

present work reports on just such a ground-breaking study. Two research objectives may be identified:

1. The study sought to describe American Adventists in terms of positions on public issues, political identification, and voting behavior. Adventists have traditionally tended to avoid socio-political questions, believing that "our kingdom is not of this world." Attention to public issues seemed to characterize "liberal" denominations that supposedly, have lost their Biblical mandate and follow a social gospel. Some exceptions to this indifference may be noted, particularly religious liberty and temperance causes—areas where Adventists have discerned moral content. But they have failed to perceive moral dimensions to most public issues.

2. The study sought to relate these socio-political attitudes and behaviors to various measures of religion in an attempt to discover if *how* Adventists are religious determines their public posture. The basic assumption is that all Adventists do not have the same religion. Under the umbrella of the church, they vary as to what they believe, how they behave, how they experience their faith, and what motivates them religiously. Do these variations make a difference in their socio-political positions?

However, even though our book is about Seventh-day Adventists, we will not begin with them. A great deal of study has convinced us that the dynamics which relate Adventists to public issues are in many ways similar to those that operate among other Christian bodies, especially evangelical Protestants. So we intend to spend some time looking at what the research has found about the relationships between religion and public policy in these widely studied groups. From this we hope to develop some theories that can help us better understand Adventist behavior.

The reverse is also true. If we could come to some understanding of how religion influences political thinking and behavior among American Seventh-day Adventists, such knowledge might well afford insights into similar relationships among other Christian communities, especially conservative ones. Perhaps the Adventist denomination might serve as a generally useful model to examine various research questions about religion and politics. While we hope that this study will prove instructive to Adventist leaders and members, we also intend for it to have a far wider audience. For the same reasons, we believe the research will be of general interest to the academic world–particularly sociologists and historians of religion. Let us begin with some definitions.

Liberals and Conservatives

The repeated use of the phrase "attitudes toward public issues" would be cumbersome. As a sort of shorthand for it, we will use "politics" or "political." Note that we are not using "politics" in its primary meaning of "the art and science of governing." Politics is ordinarily concerned with how power is employed to reach the goals and distribute the rewards of society or, according to a classic definition, "who gets what, when, and how."[10]

When we use the term, however, we are not talking about campaigning for office, steering bills through the legislative processes, making executive decisions based on popular polls, or doing deals in "smoke-filled rooms." What we ordinarily mean is how one identifies oneself in regard to a political party, how one votes, and, most of all, what one considers to be the proper course of action on important issues facing the nation which occupy the headlines of our daily newspapers. In other words, we deal with the politics, not of the professional politician, but of the common citizen.

Perhaps the most common way that scholars have explored the relationships between religion and politics has been along the conservative-liberal dimension. The conventional wisdom is that those who hold conservative religions are more conservative politically, and those who are religious liberals are more likely to be politically liberal. Before beginning to explore these dynamics, we need to have some agreement on what the terms mean.

A *conservative* is one who is inclined to preserve the existing order of things. Conservatives prize the heritage and traditions of their group and want to protect the priceless values that have been handed down to them. They are cautious about initiating change, lest the baby be thrown out with the bath water.

The word *liberal*, by contrast, comes from the root meaning "to be free." Liberals want to have an open mind to new ideas and not necessarily be bound to the way things have always been done in the past. They tend to favor "progress" and "reform" as they see it.

Defined this way, neither of these terms is pejorative, although representatives of the two ways of thinking sometimes hurl them at members of the opposite camp as if they were. Both modes of thought are necessary to human stability and progress. Going to either extreme can warp reality, and we are probably best served when they are kept in balance.

Of course, these definitions are broad and too simplistic. At times conservatives work for social change as with Ronald Reagan seeking to reverse New Deal policies or pro-life groups attempting to overthrow court rulings that permit abortion. But in seeking such change conservatives typically see themselves as going back to the values of the past. Such change is reactionary. On the other hand, when liberals resist change, they are usually contending that the status quo provides for human freedom and individual advancement. How these general attitudes actually work out to specific issues in religion and in politics is examined next.

It is also important to remember that such attitudes "are not global; they are specific to certain objects and situations. A person can be very conservative in some respects, very liberal in others . . . to classify a man or woman along a single dimension of conservative to liberal is really to average many attitudes."[11] Therefore, we do not label *people* as conservative or liberal; we attempt to describe only *positions* as such.

Now what does it mean to apply these terms to the area of religion, specifically Protestant Christianity? We should avoid dogmatic distinctions, but the most conservative position generally holds that the Bible should be taken literally, word for word, as true, that it is inerrant in the autographs, and that its specific teachings are still binding in contemporary life. An extreme liberal position may be that the Bible is merely an ancient book of legends, history, and moral teachings recorded by men which gives us insights into the religious experience of early humans. An in-between position may hold that the Bible is an inspired record of God's dealing with humankind from which we must extract universal principles to apply to contemporary situations, but that the specific applications of those principles found in Scripture are culturally conditioned and reflect the limitations of their human authors.

On this basis it is probable that few if any Seventh-day Adventists are theological liberals. Those of such persuasion would not choose to join or remain in a denomination so anchored to the Bible. Rather, those Adventists labeled liberals by their more conservative brothers and sisters are more likely to be moderates found in the in-between position. Also, few people could be described as "pure" conservatives or liberals. Christians are ranged all along the continuum.

Beliefs about the Bible and the nature of inspiration influence other areas of belief and behavior, all of which combine to make up the conservative-liberal mix. For example, Hoge, in order to test theories about denominational characteristics and church growth or decline, had twenty-five experts rate seventeen denominations on a variety of traits. These traits included theological conservatism, attitudes toward ecumenism, polity, emphasis on evangelism, involvement in social action, emphasis on distinctive life-style, and attitudes toward pluralism of beliefs.

Hoge then organized the various churches on continua ranging between the polar extremes. Interestingly, the combined ratings of the twenty-five experts placed the Seventh-day Adventist Church second most conservative in theology—just to the left of the Assemblies of God—and the second most conservative in distinctive life-style—a shade behind the Mormons.[12]

While this may be interesting, our study finally will focus not on different denominations but upon individuals within a given denomination—in this case, Seventh-day Adventism. While some churches are more liberal or conservative than others, yet a considerable range often exists among the individual members. What defines the difference?

In surveying individuals, social scientists usually attempt to determine placement on a conservative-liberal scale by employing items such as: attitude toward the Bible (as described above), attitude toward Jesus (God or great teacher), concept of Devil (personal being or myth), belief about life after death (Heaven through faith in Jesus or none), origin of human life (evolution or special creation), and belief in the miracles of Christ.[13] Since most Adventists would take a rather conservative position on these items, such a scale would probably not prove very useful in "sorting out" Adventists. Therefore, we have developed our own scale which is introduced in chapter 6.

Now what about the public life? What does political conservatism and political liberalism look like? In general, we would expect the continuum to range from conserving the best of the past to seeking new directions for the future. In real-life issues, though, the connection is not always that simple. And over time, positions tend to change. A working definition is provided by Morgan.

> In family matters, conservatives emphasize strong family ties, with dominant parents and obedient children. In education, they favor practical training as opposed to theory. In economic matters, they are for making all people 'earn their own way' and tend to favor businesspeople over labor leaders. In politics, they oppose big spending by government, object to programs of public welfare, and favor as little intervention by government as possible. They tend to be nationalistic and object to international involvements except to fight communism. They are for strict law enforcement and for severe punishment of criminals. Finally, they tend to be socially prejudiced, or racist, and status-conscious, feeling that their own kind of people are 'better' than others.[14]

Morgan goes on to say that liberal attitudes are the opposite of the conservative ones but reminds us that "each person possesses some mixture of attitudes on the various issues." Ideological identification is rarely straightforward.

The Elusive Link

As we mentioned earlier, the conservative-liberal dimension is the construct most often employed to attempt to explain the connection between religion and politics. Considerable social scientific research, with theoretical underpinning, has demonstrated that people who are "liberal" in politics tend to be more "liberal" in religion.[15]

In the Radical Right politics of the 1950s, the war against communism and other patriotic themes received vigorous support from Protestant fundamentalists like Billy James Hargis and Carl McIntire. In the 1980s, the New Religious Right strongly supported Reagan and the Republican platform including issues like the defeat of ERA, opposition to abortion, and support of prayer and Bible reading in the public schools. Of course, liberal churches have also backed political causes such as a nuclear freeze, protests against the Vietnam war, civil rights, and the Sanctuary movement.[16]

A more recent example of this connection is found in a study of the Reformed Church in America. Luidens and Nemeth discovered that support for ecumenism was related to political liberalism while support for Biblical literalism was related to political conservatism.[17]

However, other research has shown that the correlation is not quite that simple. A careful review of 266 empirical studies has revealed that the relationship is elusive with different dimensions of religion and conservatism being related in different ways.[18]

For example, Rothenberg and Newport found that evangelicalism, as defined by a variety of measures, was related to attitudes on sociopolitical issues but not strongly related to foreign policy attitudes, partisanship, or presidential voting behavior.[19]

In a study relating the importance of religion in the life to various family, political, and social attitudes that are possible consequences of religion, Hoge and Zulueta found only weak relationships except in limited areas–mostly the domains of family life, sexuality, and personal honesty. Religion had weak effects on patriotism, government involvement, and economic issues. The impact that religion did have was always in the conservative direction.[20] Hart's study of the Lutheran Church in America also reported an inconsistent relationship between conservative religion and conservative politics.[21]

Unraveling the Tangle

How can we make sense out of this conflicting information? First, we will look at some reasons why a connection between conservative religion and conservative politics might be expected. In chapter 2 we explore reasons for the inconsistencies in this relationship that have arisen in the research. Eventually, we try to fit all of this into our study of American Seventh-day Adventists.

To begin with, people with a conservative mind set may find it natural to cling to traditional ways in various areas of their lives. In religion these Christians worship a God who changes not, derive guidance from ancient Scriptures, and speak of eternal verities. Living in a world marked by rapid change in technology, learning, social arrangements, and values, they may find the church the one institution they can count on to conserve the best from the past—a pillar of stability by which to preserve order and security in their lives.

Such a mind set wants to hold on to what is tested and true, what has proved to be of value. Thus, more religiously conservative groups are more likely to support "legislation of morality" such as Sunday laws, school prayer, and regulation of intoxicating beverages.[22] From this point it is a small step to oppose communism whose aggressive atheism threatens traditional values and to favor a strong national defense to preserve American freedoms so that these values can continue. It is also easy to identify these traditional values with the capitalistic system under which they have flourished.

We might expect those Christians who hold the most orthodox beliefs—including a Biblical literalism–to be the most conservative in the political arena, basically favoring the status quo, for they have high respect for past traditions, especially those that may have resulted from divine guidance. Their use of Romans 13:1-6, for example, with its declaration that "the powers that be are ordained of God" and we should be subject to them "for conscience sake," may incline them to support the current political state regardless of how corrupt the government or how unjust its laws.

We might also expect that those members who have the greatest exposure to their faith through more frequent attendance, serving in congregational offices, taking part in witnessing activities, or studying church literature and those who manifest greater commitment by increased contributions or increased devotional activity will hold more conservative attitudes toward public issues. Having made a greater investment in their faith and having a more intelligent understanding of it, they have more to lose by changes in the status quo. We have already indicated that the relationship may well be different for Blacks and other ethnic minorities. These dynamics are discussed later in this book.

Redekop has identified three links between fundamentalist religion and right-wing political views.[23] The first is a simplistic dualism—a tendency to see everything as black or white, good or evil with no shades between. The second link is related to the first—a conspiratorial view of the world. Satan is plotting to lead people from the strait and narrow way, and communism is plotting the destruction of the traditional values that give meaning to life. There is a pulling in to defend against the common enemy.

The third link is the individualistic emphasis on salvation by fundamentalists. Salvation is a personal matter, and righteousness is seen in the vertical dimension. This matches the radical right's laissez-faire economic and social ideology. Thus, getting the heart right rather than curing the ills of society is what matters. There is low emphasis on social action which is seen to be related to the feared atheistic communism.

Related to this is the so-called Protestant ethic which encourages believers to work hard and not waste money on frivolous pleasures. The resulting prosperity and upward mobility may come to be regarded as a sign of divine favor, and the position of those less fortunate can be construed as their just desserts. Thus Christians with a more individualistic world view of religion might be expected to repudiate much of the liberal agenda and espouse much of the conservative one. Also, Christians whose images of God are the "softer" ones of mother, spouse, lover, and friend might be expected to be more supportive of a liberal social agenda and of "peace politics" than those who are more likely to conceive of God as having the sterner attributes of father, master, judge, and king.[24]

The reasonable connection between conservative-liberal religion and conservative-liberal politics is not merely one of a common way of thinking, however. It also relates to the historical development of religions within the American experience. To this topic we now turn.

References

[1]Ronald L. Johnstone, *Religion in Society*, 3rd ed. (Englewood Cliffs, NJ: Prentice Hall, 1988), 123-126.

[2]Kenneth D. Wald, "Assessing the Religious Factor in Electoral Behavior,"*Religion in American Politics*, ed. C. W. Dunn (Congressional Quarterly Press, 1989), 05-121

[3]D. A. Roozen, W. McKinney, and J. W. Carroll, *Varieties of Religious Presence: Mission in Public Life* (New York: Pilgrim Press, 1984).

[4]Johnstone, 72-76, 94-95.

[5]For a recent analysis on the restructuring of American denominations see Robert Wuthnow, *The Restructuring of*

American Religion (New Jersey: Princeton University Press, 1988), pp. 71-99.

[6]M. R. Welch and D. C. Leege, "Religious Predictors of Catholic Parishioners' Sociopolitical Attitudes: Devotional Style, Closeness to God, Imagery, and Agentic/Communal Religious Identity," *Journal for the Scientific Study of Religion* 27 (December 1988): 536-552.

[7]Stephen Hart, "Christian Faith and Nuclear Weapons: Rank-and-File Opinions," *Journal for the Scientific Study of Religion* 26 (March 1987): 38-62.

[8]J. H. Kauffman, "Dilemmas of Christian Pacifism within a Historic Peace Church," *Sociological Analysis* 49 (Winter 1989): 368-385.

[9]R. J. Nemeth and D. A. Luidens, "The New Christian Right and Mainline Protestantism: The Case of the Reformed Church in America," *Sociological Analysis* 49 (Winter 1989): 343-352.

[10]Harold Lasswell, *Politics: Who Gets What, When, and How* (New York: Meridian Books, 1958).

[11]Clifford T. Morgan, *A Brief Introduction to Psychology*, 2nd ed. (New York: McGraw-Hill Book Company, 1977), 389.

[12]Dean R. Hoge, "A Test of Theories of Denominational Growth and Decline," *Understanding Church Growth and Decline: 1950-1978*, ed. Dean Hoge and David Roozen (New York: Pilgrim Press, 1979), 179-197.

[13]Phillip E. Hammond and James Davison Hunter, "On Maintaining Plausibility: The Worldview of Evangelical

College Students," *Journal for the Scientific Study of Religion* 23 (September 1984): 221-238); see Appendix, 236-238 for items.

[14]Morgan, 389.

[15]For a sample of such research see J. K. Hadden, "An Analysis of Some Factors Associated with Religion and Political Affiliation in a College Population," *Journal for the Scientific Study of Religion* 2 (1963): 209-216; Benton Johnson, "Theology and Party Preference among Protestant Clergymen," *American Sociological Review* 31 (1966): 200-208.

[16]For a brief review of the involvement of religious groups in partisan politics in recent times see Johnstone, 128-134.

[17]Donald A. Luidens and Roger J. Nemeth, "After the Storm: Closing the Clergy-Laity Gap," *Review of Religious Research* 31 (December 1989): 183-195.

[18]Robert Wuthnow, "Religious Commitment and Conservatism: In Search of an Elusive Relationship," *Religion in Sociological Perspective*, ed. C. Y. Glock (Belmont, CA: Wadsworth Press, 1973), 117-132; see also L. R. Petersen and K. P. Takayama, "Religious Commitment and Conservatism: Toward Understanding an Elusive Relationship," *Sociological Analysis* 45 (1984): 353-371.

[19]S. Rothenberg and F. Newport, *The Evangelical Voter* (Washington, DC: Free Congress Research and Education Foundation, 1984).

[20]Dean R. Hoge and Ernesto de Zulueta, "Salience as a Condition for Various Social Consequences of Religious

Commitment," *Journal for the Scientific Study of Religion* 24 (March 1985): 21-38.

[21]Hart, 26:38-62.

[22]Johnstone, 126-127.

[23]J. H. Redekop, *The American Far Right* (Grand Rapids, MI: William B. Eerdmans, 1968).

[24]Andrew Greeley, "Religious Imagery as a Predictor Variable in the General Social Survey," paper presented to the Society for the Scientific Study of Religion, Chicago, October 1984.

Chapter 2

Made in America

When contemporary religions line up and choose sides in the political arena, this behavior can be explained, at least partly, by reference to American religious history in the nineteenth and twentieth centuries. In particular, the development of a conservative sociopolitical stance by the conservative branch of American Protestantism can be seen as a response to the challenge of modernity. We must begin by noting the phenomenon of *secularization*.

The classic understanding of secularization suggests that the hold of traditional religious values is challenged by industrialization, mass education, technological sophistication, population mobility, rapid urbanization, cultural pluralism, and the proliferation of complex forms of social organization. These developments undercut religion by rendering its theological claims less plausible and by restricting its moral impact to the realm of privately held values and orientations.[1]

Secularization operates on at least two levels. At the first, "it is assumed that there has been a displacement of religious interpretations of reality and religious orientations toward life by an orientation that seeks explanations for and justifications of human behavior and other phenomena in scientific and rational terms."[2] Thus any time we look for rational causes of things like disease, disasters, or human behavior rather than attributing them to supernatural powers such as gods or devils, we have, to at least some extent, experienced secularization.

At a second level, secularization refers to a process of increasing differentiation between the religious and the secular spheres of life. While in traditional societies, religion and public affairs have been coterminous; in modern society, life becomes segregated into private and public sectors. The private sector has to do with things like family, friends, and personal choices. The public sector deals with race, politics, economics, and national life. More and more, religion remains influential only in the private domain.[3]

Not all scholars believe, however, that secularization is an inevitable process. The modernization thesis seems to fly in the face of renewed and persistent presence of religion in the sphere of American politics. These advocates of the vitality of religion argue that the religious needs of humankind have not changed noticeably with the advent of modernity. Continual growth among new religious movements and of sectarian groups suggests that secularization, rather than being a linear process, is a self-limiting process creating religious transformation and revival.[4]

It is not our purpose to argue the point. We wish only to demonstrate how the responses to perceived secularization have influenced the development of attitudes of various branches of Christianity toward socio-political issues.

The last two centuries have witnessed remarkable advances in science and technology that have altered and even revolutionized nearly every aspect of human life. How has all of this impinged on religious belief? How has religion fared against the forces of modernity?

Responses to Modernity

In a thought-provoking study of evangelicalism in America, Hunter has identified three ways in which religion has been affected by a culture which has become increasingly enamored with the scientific method of thinking and dependent upon scientific progress. In this section, we review Hunter's interpretations.[5]

The first effect comes through the increasing *functional rationalization* of human thought. In modern society we seek to explain things which once seemed mysterious by applying natural laws. Thus the causes of disease, weather patterns, human pathology, crime and deviance, earthquakes, and flying objects are all understandable in terms of natural explanations. It is no longer necessary to postulate supernatural intervention—benevolent or malignant—to account for the unusual. We have great faith in the ability of the science and technology that can even put people on the moon and invade outer space. If something remains unexplained, we are sure that given time and money science will also unlock its mysteries. Neither God nor the devil really seem necessary.

This functional rationalization undermines the credibility of a religious world view, rendering it less plausible for the person in the street to believe in traditional Christianity. It is difficult for people to maintain strong religious attachments while living within a social structure which negates their religious heritage, particularly when their religious tradition exists in high tension with society. Thus, we might expect different levels of religious commitment among persons who have experienced different levels of rationalization.

The second effect of modernity on religion comes through *cultural pluralism*, the division of a society into subsocieties, each with its own ideologies, values, and traditions. Thus, while traditional societies usually incorporated a "state religion" with perhaps small dissenting groups on the fringes, modern America has become "the denominational society"[6] where no faith has a monopoly, but all religions must compete for their "market share" along with secular alternatives.

Cultural pluralism results from the social differentiation that takes place in the modern world as a result of urbanization, industrialization, and the spread of knowledge through the revolution in communications technology.[7] The total effect is that modern people are continually exposed to multiple world views, which are many times at odds with the religious faith in which they were reared.

Cultural pluralism is not all bad; it lies at the very foundation of religious liberty. But it puts a strain on religious faith. Since religious world views tend to be monopolistic (I have the one "true" religion), cultural pluralism weakens the plausibility structure[8] which sustains attachment to them (Nearly everybody disagrees with me. Can they *all* be wrong?).

The exposure to multiple world views as an outcome of cultural pluralism results in *cognitive dissonance*, an experience of confusion and anxiety about the certainty of one's own understanding of reality. This experience may lead to questioning or rejection of long-held beliefs or may dilute the degree of commitment to a particular understanding of faith as a result of having been exposed to other "truths." Thus, we might expect religious commitment to vary with the amount of exposure to alternative conceptions of reality other than one's own.

Hunter's third effect of modernity issues from *structural pluralism*, is the dichotomization of life into public and private spheres. In traditional societies, religion moved freely in the public realm of government, military, education, law, and medicine. In modern society religion has gradually forced to withdraw from public life (though it makes periodic comebacks as in the New Christian Right of the 1980s) and has been relegated to the private sphere.

Chapter 2

Privatization of morality is the principal constraint that structural pluralism imposes on religion. Religious symbols and authority are with-drawn from public institutions into the private sphere. Religion is depoliticized. Religious definitions of reality become less relevant in the highly rational character of the public sector. Privatization means that religion finds meaning only within the private sphere of a person's life. Obviously, this process affects the relationship between religion and politics, and to the extent that an individual or a church has bought into structural pluralism it may be expected to withdraw from the political arena.

Minority religions, including Seventh-day Adventism, foster structural pluralism for they fare better when the dominance of an "established" church has been removed. But they pay the price of seeing the wider society divorce itself from the morality that religious views of reality provide. A well-known study of individualism and commitment in American society comments on this dilemma.

> Outside this sphere of personal morality, the evangelical church has little to say about wider social commitments. Indeed, the sect draws together those who have found a personal relationship to Christ into a special loving community, and while it urgently seeks to have everyone make the same commitment, it separates its members off from attachment to the wider society. Morality becomes personal, not social; private, not public.[9]

The combined impact of these three factors is a weakening of the establishment and maintenance of the religious commitment. They contribute to what Hunter has called the *deinstitutionalization of religious reality*. By this he means "the process whereby the patterns of human behavior and social relations become unstable and the commonsense coherence of traditionally valid reality definitions become unreliable and undependable."[10] Thus while religion may persist despite these forces, it is likely to experience disaffirmation, dislocation, and reorientation leading toward a highly individualistic view of itself. It tends to withdraw into its private "shell."[11]

Hunter believes that three different reactions to the effects of modernity are possible: withdrawal, resistance, and accommodation. The first option is the least likely to be pursued by any religion because of social legitimation and church-growth interests. It cuts the church off from relevance to its times. Some small sects have taken this route, however, most notably the Amish.[12] Some individuals within any faith might also follow this path.

In most churches and with most individuals some mixture of resistance and accommodation is likely to occur. The proportions of the mixture are dependent upon the social bases, the ethical values, and the collective identity of the particular religious group—or of the individual member within the group. While some resist modernity more stoutly than others, some accommodation with the culture is inevitable from a sociological viewpoint. This is so because the plausibility structures of functional rationalization, cultural pluralism, and structural pluralism are more prevalent and far-reaching than those that help to create and maintain religious world views.

In individuals we might expect that the relative proportions of resistance and accommodation as responses of religion to modernity will determine the extent to which they engage in public issues and the direction that such engagement will take. This relationship becomes clearer when seen in historical perspective.

The Great Reversal

One of the most fascinating aspects of the development of religion vis-a-vis politics in American history is how conservative Protestantism, which once stood for involvement in society, moved gradually to a position of withdrawal and individualism as part of its response to modernity. George Marsden, whose comprehensive work we follow in this section, refers to it as "the great reversal."[13] Only in the second half of the twentieth century have the conservatives begun to re-engage in selective aspects of national life in a pattern far different from their ancestors of the eighteenth and early nineteenth centuries.

From the time of the Puritans until well into the nineteenth century, American Protestantism was dominated by a Calvinistic post-millenialism. Conservatives were the mainline Protestants in those days, largely Congregationalists, Presbyterians, and Baptists. "Liberal" groups like the Unitarians and Universalists were a small minority, the great Catholic immigrations had not yet arrived, and non-Christian groups were rare. Evangelical Protestantism reigned and believed its mission to be to usher in the Kingdom of God in America along the lines of Calvin in Geneva.[14]

This Kingdom of God would be introduced not only in the lives of the regenerate elect but also through civil laws that would restrain evil and transform society in harmony with the will of God.

> Men of seemingly sober judgment expressed repeatedly their confidence that Christians could remake society in the United States according to a pattern fashioned in heaven, and that such a restructuring of relationships would eliminate poverty, banish the curse of drunkenness, elevate womanhood, provide equal opportunity in education, and free black men from slavery. Thus they would prepare the way for the coming of Christ to rule over his kingdom.[15]

The American Republic was not only a novel experience in political freedom; it was the new promised land chosen by God.

These evangelicals did not hesitate to employ state powers for social betterment. They campaigned for prohibition as the most effective way to attack urban problems at their root, worked for national Sunday legislation, and spearheaded prison and labor reforms. They also used non-political means. By later in the 1800s, they had founded rescue missions, homes for fallen women, and relief programs. They worked among immigrants and sought jobs for large numbers of the poor. "Preaching the Gospel was always their central aim, but social and evangelistic work went hand in hand."[16]

Even when the theology of the conservative branch of Protestantism began to move toward premillenialism with its pessimistic views of the possibility of reforming society, some leaders were slow to lose their social vision. As late as 1906, William B. Riley, a leading Baptist spokesman, declared that Christians should work for democracy, elect reformers to civic office, and fight to eliminate all public vices, especially the liquor traffic. "The Church of God is especially charged with civic reform."[17] Such statements by conservatives became rare after 1910.[18]

Social concern may emphasize either or both of two methods: political means to promote the welfare of society, especially the poor and oppressed, or private charity to accomplish the same ends. Marsden points out that "the great reversal" took place in two stages. From about 1865 to 1900, interest in political action diminished among conservatives. Between 1900 and 1930, all progressive social concern, public or private, became suspect.[19]

The Rise of Individualism

Two theological trends following the Civil War accelerated the movement of evangelicalism toward a more individualistic position. The spread of holiness teaching from the pietist Methodist tradition and the introduction of dispensationalism, with its "church age," involved a shift from an Old Testament to a New Testament orientation—a shift toward a more private view of Christianity. The evangelicals gave up the "Calvinist-Puritan Old Testament covenantal view of the identity of the people of God with the advance of a religious-political kingdom."[20]

Evangelists in the later revival tradition (earlier revivalists like Charles G. Finney had linked revival with political reform) like Dwight L. Moody used the priority of evangelism as a reason to avoid emphasizing social issues. Moody both helped to set and reflected the trend away from the earlier evangelical emphasis on the direct social dimensions of sin and holiness. In his earlier ministry,

> Conversion inevitably led to personal responsibility and moral uplift, qualities which the conventional wisdom said the poor most often lacked.... Once wanderers came 'home' and the poor acquired the sense of responsibility found in strong Christian families, poverty would cease.[21]

The second theological factor in the rise of individualism was the growing acceptance of dispensationalism, usually accompanied by premillenialism. Fading was the rosy post-millenial view that the Kingdom of God was about to be inaugurated, "that change is usually, if not always, for the better, that progress is ever onward and upward, and, most important of all, that America is a nation chosen of God, a nation with a divine mission to lead mankind into the promised land."[22]

Premillenialists preached an apocalyptic message that saw the world as a "wrecked vessel," doomed to destruction before the ushering in of the new age. Nothing was to be gained by trying to improve it; the church must concentrate on trying to save lost souls out of it. Jesus Himself was no reformer, argued one, since He did not oppose slavery or war. He actually rebuked Judas for suggesting money be given to the poor. "Trying to save the world by socialism . . . was like cleaning and decorating the staterooms of a sinking ship."[23]

To look at it another way, the conservative shift to individualism may be summed under three points: (1) A pessimistic assessment of human culture and its achievements in light of the fall which suggested that society was not susceptible to improvement; (2) view of separation of church and state that held that the church should not involve itself, even to issuing pronouncements, in government affairs; (3) understanding that the primary contribution of Christianity to culture was the fostering of right belief for moral action must always proceed from right doctrine.

Protestants at War

In addition to the factors discussed, part of the "great reversal" must be explained by the fundamentalist reaction to the liberal social gospel after 1900. In the latter part of the nineteenth century Protestantism found itself having to deal with issues which challenged traditional faith—especially Darwinism and Biblical criticism. In line with our earlier discussion of possible responses to modernity, those who did more resisting became the fundamentalist branch while those who did more accommodating became the liberal—and eventually the mainline—branch of Protestantism.

While the struggle was long and fierce, splitting denominations, "American evangelicalism was becoming a movement of the disinherited."[24] Once the mainline group, conservatives now found themselves in an increasingly beleaguered position. Their ethical rigor shifted from efforts to transform the culture toward constructing symbols of separation.

Meanwhile, those Christians who were more likely to accommodate to modernity—especially those who had been most influenced by functional rationalization—saw God revealed in a cultural development that harmonized with social evolution. By definition, the greater the functional rationality, the more likely that adherents will demythologize the supernatural elements of their world view and will increase their attempts to provide rational explanations for their beliefs. Human society was moving toward the realization of the Kingdom of God; the spiritual progress of the Kngdom could be seen in the progress of culture. "Social Christianity" became thoroughly identified with liberalism and thus was viewed with suspicion by the conservatives.

> The threat that conservative evangelicals perceived in the Social Gospel was not that it endorsed social concerns—evangelicals themselves often made similar endorsements. It was rather that the Social Gospel emphasized social concern in an exclusivistic way which seemed to undercut the relevance of the message of salvation through trust in

Christ's atoning work. . . . The Social Gospel was presented, or was thought to be presented, as equivalent to the Gospel itself.[25]

So liberals used social action to forward the progress of civilization and thus to hasten the Kingdom of God. Fundamentalists now clung to a premillenial eschatological hope. And because the Social Gospel and the progressive movement in politics were strongly related, fundamentalists rejected them both. On the eve of America's entry into World War I, an article in the conservative journal *Our Hope* declared that "Christians should separate themselves from the world, should not enter politics nor vote, and should not 'set out to improve the world.'"[26]

Another Switch

World War I marked the beginning of another change for fundamentalists. Since much of Biblical criticism had originated in Germany and since the fundamentalists' patriotism had been questioned by the liberals, the fundamentalists, due to their apolitical stance, went on the offensive. Their strongest line of attack on modernism was found to be a position which put forward the survival of civilization from godless forces as a principal concern. They found themselves in the paradox of holding, as premillenialists, that there was no hope for the culture but at the same time saying, as traditional Americans, that a return to Christian principles was the only hope for the nation. The paradox remains today.

The World's Christian Fundamentals Association, organized after the war, expressed strong concern for the condition of American society. However, this concern was not expressed in the liberal vein of social action but in the battle against enemies who would threaten traditional values and in the pressure for morality legislation. The anti-German theme was joined with evolution and modernism, and the package was touted as both a religious and a cultural threat.

> Out of these concerns, to which anti-communism was soon added, fundamentalist super-patriotism began to grow. Thus a movement that had characteristically claimed that loyalty was not owed to kings and nations, and had been sufficiently apolitical in 1917 to be suspected of disloyalty, became sufficiently patriotic to make the defense of Christian civilization in America one of its major goals.[27]

As we noted in chapter 1, this disposition peaked in the Radical Right politics of the 1950s and again in the New Christian Right of the 1980s. It is not hard to see how the Protestant ethic of individualism finds affinity with the political system of capitalism. Both place priority on individual rather than societal problems, and both look for individual solutions. And since the fundamentalists are pointing toward other-worldly resolutions for social problems, they do not disturb the comfortable status quo of the contemporary capitalist culture.

Chapter 2

As early as 1921, a writer in the liberal *Christian Century* sarcastically pointed out the connection: "When the capitalist discovers a brand of religion which has not the slightest interest in 'the social gospel,' but on the contrary intends to pass up all reforms to the Messiah who will return on the clouds of heaven, he has found just the thing he has been looking for."[28]

Fundamentalism as such lost the battle of the 1920s and 1930s. Today, a relatively small number of conservative Protestants would identify themselves as fundamentalists. Many of their basic themes live on, however, in the large and influential group of neo-evangelicals. While mainline liberal churches—so successful in the first half of the twentieth century—have been losing membership in the last few decades, conservative evangelicals have been growing and may well represent the mainline churches of tomorrow.[29] Like the evangelicals of an earlier day, they are interested and involved in public issues. Unlike their spiritual forebears, they seek to preserve the political and social system rather than to challenge it. Where once theological conservatism was associated with political liberalism, it is now related to political conservatism.

The enigma remains: How can premillenialists, who believe in the irreparable nature of culture and whose hope is in the apocalyptic coming of the King, embrace a highly politicized gospel of super-patriotism, anti-communism, and the preservation of traditional societal values? Marsden suggests that the answer might lie in an understanding of the fundamentalist mentality which tends to see this world as an arena of conflict between the forces of good and the forces of evil.

While other Christian bodies have also seen in history a struggle between God and Satan, fundamentalists are disposed to dichotomize *all* reality into the saved and the lost, the true and the false, etc. No "in-between" exists to confuse the mind.

Prior to the first World War fundamentalists had developed little political theory. In the years following, as communist and other conspiracy theories arose, the fundamentalists had to incorporate them into their cosmic scheme. These conspiracy theories harmonized well with their stark dualism.

> Like their premillenialism, the political threats could be placed in the framework of the conflict between the forces of God and of Satan. The two types of conspiracy theory, the political and the religious, might well have appealed to a single mind-set in such a way as to override the difficulty of reconciling specific details.
>
> ... It seemed consistent then for some fundamentalists to conclude also that Satan's hosts would appear in clearly identifiable political manifestations, just as they appeared so clearly in the churches and schools [a reference to the conflict over the teaching of evolution highlighted by the famous Scopes 'monkey trial' of 1925]. In the face of this threat, the political battle to defend God's kingdom could not be entirely postponed until a coming era.[30]

Chapter 2

It is somewhat of a paradox that the rise of individualism in religion is not simply a reaction against modernity but, in some ways, an accommodation to it. The general disinterest of conservative Christian groups (including Adventism) in political issues with its accompanying lack of social involvement has traditionally been defended on theological grounds and practical considerations (diversion from winning converts) as sketched above. However, quite imperceptibly and subtly, their reaction also has much to do with "accommodation" to the forces of modern society, particularly structural pluralism. These forces lead religionists to individualize and compartmentalize their religious life. Thus while the conservative disengagement is on the surface a defense of orthodoxy, it actually contains elements of a very secularized reaction.

Is it possible to put all the information in this and in chapter 1 together in such a way as to offer a reasonably accurate prediction as to how variability in religious beliefs and behaviors might influence positions on public issues? The task is not easy, but let us make an attempt.

References

[1] For example, see David Martin, *A General Theory of Secularization* (New York: Harper & Row, 1978); Bryan Wilson, *Contemporary Transformations of Religion* (London: Oxford University Press, 1976).

²Ronald L. Johnstone, *Religion in Society*, 3rd ed. (Engelwood Cliffs, NJ: Prentice Hall, 1988), 271; see section from 271-275.

³Joseph B. Tamney and Stephen D. Johnson, "Consequential Religiosity in Modern Society," *Review of Religious Research* 26 (June 1985): 360-378; see also Bryan Wilson, *Contemporary Transformations of Religion* (London: Oxford Press, 1976).

⁴Rodney Stark and William Sims Bainbridge, *The Future of Religion* (Berkeley, CA: University of California Press, 1985). See also Robert Wuthnow, *The Restructuring of American Religion* (New Jersey: Princeton University Press, 1988) and Wade Clark Roof and William McKinney, *American Mainline Religion* (New Brunswick, N.J.: Rutgers University Press, 1987).

⁵James Davison Hunter, *American Evangelicalism: Conservative Religion and the Quandary of Modernity* (New Brunswick, NJ: Rutgers University Press, 1983). See also James Davison Hunter, *Evangelicalism: The Coming Generation* (Chicago: Chicago University Press, 1987).

⁶Andrew M. Greeley, *The Denominational Society* (Glenview, IL: Scott, Foresman, and Co., 1972).

⁷See Harvey Cox, *The Secular City* (New York: Macmillan, 1965).

⁸See Peter L. Berger, *The Sacred Canopy* (Garden City, NY: Doubleday, 1969), 46. Berger uses the term "plausibility structure" to mean a network of persons sharing a meaning system such as a particular religion. The meaning system

continues to be plausible (i.e., believable) only within this network but is disconfirmed outside of it.

[9]Robert Bellah, Richard Madsen, William Sullivan, Ann Swidler, and Steven Tipton, *Habits of the Heart* (Berkeley, CA: University of California Press, 1985), 231.

[10]Hunter, 14.

[11]For similar conclusions see Roof and McKinney, 40-72.

[12]See Donald B. Kraybill, *The Riddle of Amish Culture* (Baltimore: Johns Hopkins University Press, 1989).

[13]George M. Marsden, *Fundamentalism and American Culture: The Shaping of Twentieth-Century Evangelicalism: 1870-1925* (New York: Oxford University Press, 1980), 85-86. The term first appeared in David O. Moberg, *The Great Reversal* (New York: A. J. Holman Company, 1977).

[14]See H. Richard Niebuhr, *The Kingdom of God in America* (New York: Harper & Row, 1937); Martin E. Marty, *Righteous Empire* (New York: Dial Press, 1970).

[15]Timothy L. Smith, "Social Reform: Some Reflections on Causation and Consequence," in *The Rise of Adventism: Religion and Society in Mid-Nineteenth-Century America*, ed. Edwin S. Gaustad (New York: Harper & Row, 1974), 18.

[16]Marsden, 84.

[17]Quoted in Marsden, 128.

[18]For a recent review see Norris Magnuson, *Salvation in*

the Slums: Evangelical Social Work, 1865-1920 (Grand Rapids, MI: Baker Book House, 1990).

[19] Marsden, 86.

[20] Ibid., 88.

[21] Ibid., 37.

[22] William G. McLoughlin, "Revivalism," in *The Rise of Adventism: Religion and Society in Mid-Nineteenth-Century America*, ed. Edwin S. Gaustad (New York: Harper & Row, 1974), 131.

[23] Marsden, 126.

[24] Ibid., 32.

[25] Ibid., 92.

[26] Ibid., 144.

[27] Ibid., 152.

[28] Quoted in ibid., 206.

[29] Dean M. Kelley, *Why Conservative Churches Are Growing: A Study in Sociology of Religion*, 2nd ed. (San Francisco: Harper and Row, 1977). For a more recent discussion on the present and future changes of American mainline denominations see Wade Clark Roof and William McKinney, *American Mainline Religion* (New Brunswick, N.J.: Rutgers University Press, 1987).

[30] Marsden, 211.

Chapter 3

The Jewel of Consistency

If this discussion so far seems to be a bit confusing and difficult to "get a handle on," the reader is encouraged not to lose heart. This subject *is* complex, but its complexity doesn't diminish its importance. After all, the resolution of the public issues of the day affects the quality of the world in which we live. Though subjects of a heavenly kingdom, we also occupy a lifetime on this planet in human society. Thus, the key question of this inquiry becomes: Does our religion make a difference in this temporal world? It seems to us that this is a question with which we should not and cannot avoid grappling.

In an attempt to bring clarity to this morass of material, Lovin suggests that the relationship between faith and public life may be summarized under three basic claims. Religion maintains order, guarantees freedom, and provides for the possibility for new forms of social justice.[1] "Religion, then, relates not only to the specific policy questions that come into public dispute, but also to the underlying beliefs about order, freedom, or justice in which the policy discussions are set."[2] We now turn to these considerations.

Order, Freedom, and Justice

In order for any human society to function, it must have a system of laws or agreed-upon behaviors and some type of government to administer these laws. Where no rules exist, anarchy results. But the human being is basically self-centered. Why should people surrender their self-interests for the common good? Of course, superior power and threat of punishment might be used to keep people in line, but it takes a huge police apparatus to rule by force alone, and authoritarian governments tend regularly to be overthrown.

Actually, governments are most successful in maintaining their positions when they can claim some sort of moral authority which legitimates their right to rule. The governing body "must inspire a primitive awe that paves the way for cooperation and obedience, but it must also convey the impression that this power is in service of some worthy ideal, such as justice or the common good, and not simply an extension of the whim of the ruler."[3]

While a number of routes may lead to this end, religion has been historically the most powerful legitimating force for it places its claims to authority on sacred and supernatural forces. Thus we have the "divine right of kings" philosophy of the early modern era. Religion provides a comprehensive framework of shared meanings—in a nonpluralistic society—that serves as a unifying force for the common good.

The first function of religion, then, is to maintain order, to keep society from crumbling, and to preserve the worthwhile values upon which that society is built.[4] This is usually a conservative function as illustrated in the efforts of the New Christian Right with its Moral Majority to define and maintain community standards or in the drive of fundamentalists to support the American capitalistic system and defeat the rival atheistic communism. However, it could take a more liberal tack such as those do who promote "civil religion," a set of shared religious and quasi-religious symbols that transcend denominational differences and are employed to promote a unifying nationalism.

The function of maintaining order leads churches to support all kinds of "legislation of morality." Some examples in American history are Sunday laws, prohibition, outlawing the teaching of evolution in the schools, an amendment to allow prayer and Bible reading in public schools, and the public control of abortion. Under this formulation, much talk occurs concerning the threat to civilization by the collapse of the old value system, and the "righteous" gear for battle against the conspiracies of humanism, secularism, atheism, and communism.

Since the days of Roger Williams in Puritan America, however, a second basic function of religion has run parallel to and in tension with that of maintaining order. By many, religion's guarantee of freedom has been seen as its most important contribution to public life. People of many different persuasions came to these shores in order to assert the freedom to live their own particular faiths. Such liberty became explicit in the first amendment to the U. S. Constitution. It may also be observed in the "higher law" concept by which reformers challenge the established order. One example is the American abolitionist movement of the nineteenth century.

In America this ideal was demonstrated in denominationalism. No established church would be allowed, but each group could form its own sect and worship as it pleased. Under the function of freedom we see "none of the appeal to shared cultural meanings that marks 'civil religion.' The system of meanings which makes morality possible belongs to the gathered community, to those who explicitly identify themselves with the faith that preserves the religious meanings."[5]

Obviously, the functions of order and of freedom must often clash. For example, to some, Sunday laws preserve an important value and strengthen the existing social order while to others they threaten the freedom to worship according to the dictates of conscience.

> That is to say that what the advocates of freedom most fear is precisely what the

partisans of order want: a single system of meanings to which everyone in the culture may and must subscribe, which gains its power to guide and motivate action by overshadowing more particular commitments with its own impression of ultimate reality and power.[6]

The struggle for religious liberty is aided by the presence of religious pluralism. As long as a number of religious bodies exist and thrive, "no totalitarian power can plausibly claim that there are no centers of meaning and value outside of its own ideology."[7] Also this freedom is best preserved by separation of church and state. When the church takes care of its own business within its own community, it is less likely to provoke the conflict that may lead to attempts to incorporate it into the larger order.

Logically, we may think of order as being a priority for conservative religions and freedom as supported by liberal ones. This may be true if the conservative groups are large and powerful and have the possibility of establishing control, as the New Christian Right of the 1980s thought it did. The situation is different, however, when the conservative religion is a minority in high tension with surrounding society, as Seventh-day Adventists have been throughout their history in America. Here a theologically conservative group may prize liberty over the order that they perceive may be used against them. Thus, their liberal opposition to Sunday laws and state-sponsored prayer in public schools.

The third function described by Lovin moves from preservation, whether of larger societal or smaller group values, to social change. Illustrated by the nineteenth-century abolitionists, the Social Gospel movement, or the Civil Rights agitation, this function points to religion as faith in the possibility of social justice. Churches or their representatives have mounted campaigns of public persuasion and have attempted to influence litigation and legislation to introduce values that seem vital according to their understanding of religious reality but which are not being endorsed in the current society.

> The critical challenges for the future of public life arise not when disagreements within a framework of shared meanings test the limits of government's capacity to keep order without destroying freedom, but when it becomes apparent that no framework of concepts or concrete social structures exists in which the justice that a group's self-understanding demands can be recognized by the wider society.[8]

Such religious claims are based on an understanding of the basic human problem as more than just individual sinfulness but involving a breakdown of communal relationships. The solution is not merely the rescue of individual sinners from this world but a healing of the brokenness of society. Regardless of what the afterlife may hold, the Christian's duty, according to this view, is to work for the establishment of the Kingdom of Heaven here and now.

Representatives of "religion for justice" realize that their vision of ultimate reality differs from many in society, but they believe that above group-specific values lie transcendent abstract-universal values. It is their calling to raise the consciousness of their fellow citizens to an awareness of those principles of justice, fairness, and human dignity that transcend mere denominational differences. While this function has been most often associated with theological liberalism (in this century), it harks back to the Old Testament concept of the covenant community.

A Series of Hypotheses

We have examined a great deal of both historical and theoretical material linking religion and politics. All of this should allow us to make some predictions about what particular religious beliefs, behaviors, feelings, and motivations should produce corresponding attitudes toward public issues. While the connections are anything but simple, and human behavior in general defies the precise predictability of laboratory science, we lay out here a series of hypotheses which we can later test with the use of our data on Seventh-day Adventists.

1. Christians who hold conservative theological beliefs, especially the inerrancy[9] and literalism of the Biblical record, are likely to have a mind set that values the heritage of the past and, therefore, is cautious and resistant about change. This may carry over into a desire to preserve the values of society and lead to conservative political positions especially as these concern public morality and defense of the political and economic system of their country.

2. Christians whose beliefs encourage a dualistic world view where the struggle between Christ and Satan is an ongoing process and where evil forces are in

Chapter 3

conspiracy against the government of God are likely to take a militant stand against forces perceived to be part of that conspiracy such as communism, Catholicism, humanism, etc.

3. Such conservative Christians are likely to view the threatening forces as having captured the more liberal churches through the influence of evolution and higher criticism. They wish to distance themselves from anything so tainted. Since liberal churches long have been identified with social action, conservatives may reject such action, seeing it as undermining the genuine Gospel. This distancing may result in withdrawal from the public arena or, if the conspiracy seems too intense, active engagement on behalf of the conservative agenda.

4. Where such threats to traditional societal values are perceived as great, conservative Christians are likely to enter the arena on the side of *order*, promoting legislation to regulate morality and to defend traditional structures, *unless* the conservatives are in too small a minority to have a chance to work their will. In this case they may champion *freedom*.

5. Those conservative Christians whose beliefs stem from a pietism that tends to see the human dilemma and solution in terms of individual sinfulness and individual salvation tend not to support social *justice* causes. The *privatization* of religion inclines toward a lack of interest in public issues since religion is seen as largely a personal and family matter.

6. Conservative Christians with premillenial beliefs are likely to avoid public issues since the world is a "wrecked vessel" that no amount of social action can improve. Since the planet will soon end in catastrophe, Christians should concentrate on saving people out of

it. However, such Christians may take action to hold back conspiratorial forces in order to allow the Gospel of individual salvation to be preached.

7. Religious belief and religious practice are related, especially among conservatives. Therefore, those Christians who more fully participate in church functions, who are more committed to the church as an institution, and who engage more often in devotional practices recommended by the church are likely to exhibit the same behaviors described above as those with strong orthodox beliefs.

8. Those with more liberal theological views are likely to possess a mind set more willing to experiment with political and economic changes as possible solutions to societal problems.

9. Liberal Christians tend to be more optimistic about the prospects of making structural improvements in society and thus are more likely to employ social and political action and to work for social *justice*.

10. Since liberal Christians tend to accommodate rather than resist modernity, they do not perceive conspiracy and threats in those who differ from them. Thus, they are more likely to de-emphasize the function of *order* and to encourage pluralism through championing *freedom*.

11. Christians whose religious orientation tends to be open and tentative rather than fixed and dogmatic–whether the content of their beliefs is conservative or liberal–are more likely to favor liberal political positions.

12. Whatever the factors that establish a connection between religion and politics–class, social status, theology, etc.–the connection has a tendency to become relatively permanent. "The political traditions of

religious communities, once established, form an important part of their members' sense of identity and tend, like religion itself, to be passed on from parents to children."[10]

One complicating factor should be mentioned. While it is reasonably easy to classify a theological teaching as liberal or conservative, the distinction is a bit trickier when it comes to political issues. The shifting sands of time frequently change the distinguishing marks. For example, in America the conservative forces originally favored strong central government, and liberals favored states' rights. By the New Deal days of the 1930s, this had turned around.

In another shift, Republicans were the advocates of civil rights for Blacks following the Civil War. But the distinctive forces of American history have now assigned that role to Democrats.

Closer to the thrust of our study is the question of whether establishing normal, peaceful relations with the Soviet Union (a political reality at the time of data collection) is a conservative position or not. Throughout much of the history of Soviet Russia certainly it would not have been. Based on Marxist atheism, attempting to address human problems by means of state-mandated socialism, and aggressive to extend its hegemony, the "evil empire" was railed against by all good fundamentalists and super patriots. Yet in the 1980s, the most conservative United States president in fifty years cautiously established a friendship with Russia. And conservatives could reason that such detente lessened the threat of nuclear war and thus helped to preserve their traditional heritage. All of this makes it a bit more difficult to find order and consistency in our proposed hypotheses.

The Search for Consistency

Just when we think we have developed a logical and defensible theory, we find to our dismay that the actual behavior of people does not always fit neatly into our scheme. Thus, as mentioned in chapter 1, the expected relations are not always found among evangelicals, Lutherans, and other religious groups. And even where the theoretical connections hold, the magnitude of the relationships has tended to be weak. Why, oh why, can't people be more consistent!

Some relief may come from a brief look at *cognitive consistency theory*. The basic idea is that "an attitude provides some consistency for response tendencies that otherwise would be incongruous or inconsistent."[11]

This theory is actually a family of consistency theories such as balance, congruity, symmetry, dissonance, etc. which have in common the concept that people tend to act in ways that minimize the internal inconsistency among their interpersonal relations, among their conflicting thoughts, or among their beliefs, feelings, and actions.[12] The individual strives for some type of consistency between his/her belief system and overt behavior and seeks some balance among the conflicting demands of social environment, interpersonal relationships, and personal needs.[13]

People may maintain consistency by averaging together a number of conflicting attitudes toward something to arrive at a single less complex attitude, or they may revise attitudes to bring them into line with commitments they have already chosen.[14] The important thing is that no matter how confused and inconsistent a person's attitudes and behaviors may seem to us, the individual has found a way to make them harmonize in his/her mind.

Kiecolt and Nelsen have attempted to apply this theory to the religious-political connection.[15] They note that in the 1960s, Johnson reported that a greater proportion of liberal Protestants were consistent on political issues than were conservative Protestants. His interpretation was that social issues have less religious significance for conservatives than they do for liberals. Since conservatives are less likely to be engaged in the political arena, their attitudes toward public issues are less consistent.[16]

This judgment may have seemed appropriate at the time since the 1960s represent a highwater mark for political liberalism. It was liberal clergy who marched in the Civil Rights Movement and protested the Vietnam War. But in the mid-70s, liberal churches, faced with declining memberships, began to lose their political momentum. By the 1980s, it was the conservatives, led by televangelists like Jerry Falwell, who were rippling the political waters.[17] With conservatives more active, would theological liberals still prove to be more politically consistent?

Kiecolt and Nelsen hold that "consistency among issue beliefs presupposes a level of sophistication in political thinking that often is not attained."[18] That is, an individual may be attracted to a particular issue but not be aware of where it fits on a conservative-liberal continuum or, for that matter, not see it in terms of ideology at all.

To test this concept, Kiecolt and Nelsen employed the two dimensions of *level of conceptualization* and *political belief system consistency*. The first refers to the degree of abstraction in political thinking.

> At the top level are '*ideologues*,' individuals who base their candidate and party preferences on a liberal-conservative 'yardstock' [sic] that serves to structure their opinions on issues. The second level contains individuals who base their political decision-making on '*group benefits*,' that is, whether their group is likely to be helped or hurt.[19]

Next come *nature of the times* citizens who respond to isolated issues or short-term concerns. At the bottom is the *no issue content* level where preferences are apolitical or without apparent rhyme or reason.

Political belief consistency refers to the degree to which individuals consistently take conservative or liberal positions on issues. One would expect that consistency would decrease with descending levels of conceptualization. The authors tested the hypothesis with data drawn from the American National Election Studies of 1972, 1980, and 1984.

True to expectations, the researchers found that consistency is greatest among the ideologues and decreases with lower levels of conceptualization. They also discovered proportionately more ideologues among liberal than among conservative Protestants and, in addition, somewhat less belief system consistency among conservatives than among liberals at all levels of conceptualization. Thus, in general, conservatives were "less likely to link issues to the left/right political ideology in which political conflicts are framed" suggesting "a somewhat lower level of psychological involvement of the conservative Protestant mass public in the political arena."[20]

Thus, in spite of the recent increase in political involvement on the part of evangelicals, they do not seem to be as consistent in fitting their positions on individual issues into a larger theoretical framework as do the liberals. The conservative mind set seems to run more toward concrete issues than toward integrated ideology.

So why do the effects of religious beliefs on political attitudes seem small–and sometimes even contradictory? In grappling with this conundrum, Jelen has suggested three summary reasons:

1. Religion may be a specialized short-term force which attains political importance only in restricted circumstances–such as the 1960 and 1980 presidential elections.

2. A lack of sophistication on the part of those with conservative religion may prevent them from perceiving how their religious beliefs are relevant to contemporary political choices (the Kiecolt-Nelsen argument).

3. Fundamentalism (the most conservative branch of evangelical Protestantism) embraces a "doctrine of separation" against theological liberalism and contemporary culture. Thus, it may, except on the more obvious moral issues, avoid "worldly entanglements" like politics. That is, these Christians may need to maintain an apolitical self-image although, in fact, they have to make political choices.[21]

As we attempt to apply the theoretical framework developed in the first three chapters to the experience of Seventh-day Adventists, we encounter some additional problems. All of the intertwined complexities we have seen in the Protestant world at large also affect the relationship between religion and politics among Adventists. But on top of these, Adventists have some special determinants which arise out of their unique history in America. To these we must now address ourselves.

References

[1] Robin W. Lovin, "Religion and American Public Life: Three Relationships," in *Religion and American Public Life*, ed. Robin W. Lovin (New York: Paulist Press, 1986), 7-28. The following section is based on Lovin's paper.

[2] Ibid., 9.

[3] Ibid., 10.

[4] For an extensive discussion on the cohesive function of religion see Meredith B. McGuire, *Religion: The Social Context*, 3rd ed. (Belmont, CA: Wadsworth, 1992), 175-209.

[5] Lovin, "Religion and American Public Life: Three Relationships," 15.

[6] Ibid., 16-17.

[7]Ibid., 17.

[8]Ibid., 20.

[9]Inerrancy of the Biblical record is not the official position of the Seventh-day Adventist Church. However, Adventists hold a very high view of inspiration, and it is likely that many members, lacking sophistication in textual backgrounds, are not able to grasp the difference between inerrancy of text and infallibility of message.

[10]Benton Johnson, "Religion and Politics in America: The Last Twenty Years," in Phillip E. Hammond, *The Sacred in a Secular Age* (Berkeley, CA: University of California Press, 1985), 303.

[11]Clifford T. Morgan, *A Brief Introduction to Psychology*, 2nd ed. (New York: McGraw-Hill Book Company, 1977), 381.

[12]See Shel Feldman, ed., *Cognitive Consistency: Motivational Antecedents and Behavioral Consequents* (New York: Academic Press, 1966).

[13]See R. P. Abelson, E. Aronson, W. J. McGuire, T. M. Newcomb, M. J. Rosenburg, and P. H. Tannenbaum, eds., *Theories of Cognitive Consistency: A Sourcebook* (Chicago: Rand McNally, 1968).

[14]Morgan, 381-382.

[15]K. Jill Kiecolt and Hart M. Nelson, "The Structuring of Political Attitudes among Liberal and Conservative Protestants," *Journal for the Scientific Study of Religion* 27 (March 1988): 48-59.

[16] Benton Johnson, "Theology and the Position of Pastors on Public Issues," *American Sociological Review* 32 (1967): 433-442.

[17] See Benton Johnson, "Religion and Politics in America," 305-310.

[18] Kiecolt and Nelsen, *op. cit.*, 50.

[19] Ibid.

[20] Ibid., 57-58.

[21] Ted G. Jelen, "The Effects of Religious Separatism on White Protestants in the 1984 Presidential Election," *Sociological Analysis* 48 (1987): 30-45.

Chapter 4

Adventism and Politics in Historical Perspective

In considering the historical relationship of the Seventh-day Adventist Church to the United States government, Jonathan Butler has identified three phases. In their Millerite beginnings and very early days, Adventists espoused an *apolitical apocalyptic* in which they avoided any relation to government. From mid-century until the 1870s, they moved to a *political apocalyptic* in which they denounced the Republic as doomed, using the language of contemporary politics. By the 1880s and beyond, they adopted a *political prophetic* which "engaged them as prophets to sustain the Republic, at least for a time, rather than merely to forecast its ruin as apocalyptists."[1]

The Early Years

The followers of William Miller were caught up in one great cause–the imminent coming of Jesus. Within months or days their Lord would appear on the clouds of heaven to bring an end to this age, including all temporal governments. To spend time on current public issues simply didn't make sense. The Kingdom was at the door.

A number of the Millerite leaders had been active in humanitarian causes prior to their commitment to preaching the Second Advent. For example, Joseph Bates had helped to organize both a temperance society and an anti-slavery society. But once swept up in preaching the soon coming of Christ, Bates found no time or energy for these former pursuits. He reasoned that those who accepted the Advent teaching would live temperate lives and oppose slavery naturally so it would be most effective to work at the fountain head of morality. Other Millerites generally adopted this attitude.[2]

After the disappointment of 1844, those Millerites who clung to their faith in the time prophecy and adopted the seventh-day Sabbath spent the next few years trying to agree on a core of doctrines and establish a sense of identity as a religious group. While Christ had not returned at the predicted time, they still expected His coming to be very soon and put all their efforts into attaining a state of readiness. They would not recognize government, even to the point of organizing as a legal entity, for they felt that any such bow to societal arrangements would constitute them as Babylon. They were "*apolitical apocalyptics* in that they spurned even minimal political participation as they awaited an imminent end."[3]

The first actual engagement with government came over the hotly debated matter of church organization. James White defended the need to organize by, in part, arguing that while the believers in 1844 had considered the beast of Revelation 13 to be a symbol of earthly government and voting or holding civil office to be receiving his mark, they had come to a better understanding of the identity of the beast, and these earlier positions were now untenable. Thus, incorporating with the state would not be a denial of faith.[4] White's logic carried the day, and the new church was legally incorporated.

The foundation for the shift to a *political apocalyptic* had been laid even earlier, however. In 1851, just about the time that Sabbath-keeping Adventists had defined their basic doctrines, established a sense of identity, and begun to institutionalize with the establishment of publications, a new interpretation of prophecy was introduced. Twenty-two-year-old scholar, John N. Andrews, published what was to become a unique Adventist view of the American government.[5]

While many Protestant interpreters had held that the first beast of Revelation 13 represented the papacy, Andrews went on to apply the second beast in the chapter–the one with two horns like a lamb but who spoke as a dragon–to the United States of America.

Andrews pioneered in arguments which were to become standard for Adventist evangelists, using such features as the location of the power and the manner, place, and time of its appearance. He held the horns to be symbolic of its Republican civil power and its Protestant ecclesiastical power. To "speak like a dragon" would be to repudiate its principles and to enforce the worship of the first beast upon its citizens.

Thus the foundation was early laid to view the American Republic as the ultimate persecuting enemy. While Adventists would follow the New Testament counsel to be good citizens and obey government as long as its dictates did not conflict with their duty to God, they would view government suspiciously, realizing that at any time the dragon might cast off its lamblike disguise. For the next few decades, pronouncements about government tended to follow this *political apocalyptic*. This is most evident in the matter of slavery and the Civil War.

Slavery and the Civil War

The American Civil War of 1861-1865 with its connection to the moral status of slavery provided the newly organized Seventh-day Adventist Church its first real opportunity to become involved in important contemporary public issues. Church leaders did speak out rather forcefully on this national problem. So much so, in fact, that some have seen the contrast between the activist stance of the church of the 1860s and the low profile of the church during the Civil

Rights movement of the 1960s as indicative of a shift in the way the church views itself in the public realm.[6]

In an attempt to demonstrate the social activism of our pioneers within their culture, Roy Branson pointed out that abolition was a minority position for dealing with the slavery problem both before and during the early years of the war. Even in the North abolitionists were likely to be ostracized and sometimes threatened (William Lloyd Garrison was mobbed in Boston). Branson has assembled evidence to show that, in spite of this, Adventists generally stood with the abolitionists. For example, Joseph Bates helped to found an abolitionist society in his home town; John P. Kellogg harbored fleeing slaves on his Michigan farm; John Byington, first president of the General Conference, maintained a station of the Underground Railroad at his home in Buck's Bridge, New York; and abolitionist and former slave, Sojourner Truth, was closely associated with Adventists in Battle Creek.[7]

Ellen White wrote extensively on the evils of slavery. She called it "a sin of the darkest dye"[8] and counseled church members to disobey the Fugitive Slave Law.[9] She complained that the war should have had as its object the freeing of the slaves, not merely the preservation of the Union.[10] And she called the national days of prayer and fasting for victory an "insult to Jehovah" while the nation continued in its sin of slavery.[11]

In 1862, before emancipation was declared, editor Uriah Smith censured President Lincoln for "following his present conservative, not to say suicidal, policy" of attempting to win the war without freeing the slaves.[12] John Andrews objected to those members who felt that

Chapter 4

their religious beliefs should not inform their behavior concerning slavery because this was a matter of "politics" which should not be mixed with religion.

> Should the All-seeing Judge, however, inquire into their connection with this great iniquity, they suppose the following answer will be entirely satisfactory to Him: 'I am not at all censurable for anything said or done by me in behalf of slavery; for O Lord, Thou knowest, it was a part of my politics!' Will this plea be offered by any reader of this article?[13]

Before concluding that the Adventist church of the 1860s was actively working to abolish slavery and establish a just society, however, we must notice some complicating factors. The antislavery position remained mostly rhetoric–Adventists did not generally work for abolition, serve in the army, or, in the majority of cases, even vote. Those individuals mentioned above who did take some action were mostly involved before they became active Seventh-day Adventists, as noted with Joseph Bates.

More importantly, the condemnation of slavery was not so much an effort to abolish the institution as it was to illustrate the dragon-like characteristics of the United States. James White applied the actions of the second beast of Revelation 13, which had a lamblike appearance but spoke like a dragon, to the nation's practice of holding four million human beings in "the most abject and cruel bondage and servitude."[14] In a chapter on "The Sins of Babylon," Ellen White cited the defense of slavery by churches as proof that they were a part of apostate Babylon.[15]

Adventists at this time did not believe society could be reformed and supposed that slavery would persist until the coming of Christ. Therefore, their rhetoric was not to bring about change but to alert people to the fulfilling prophecies of Revelation and thus to the nearness of the end. In an unsigned editorial prior to the election of 1856, where the issues of slavery were clearly drawn, Uriah Smith explained why Adventists would not participate:

> To the question, why we do not with our votes and influence labor against the evil tendency of the times, we reply, that our views of prophecy lead us to the conclusion that things will not be bettered. This country, if we are correct in believing it to be symbolized by the two-horned beast of Rev. xiii, will finally sustain such an abominable character that it will be landed in the Lake of fire. Rev. xix, 20. The two-horned beast *will* speak like a dragon. Rev. xiii, 11. We do not therefore feel it incumbent upon us to labor, in this respect, either to hasten or retard the fulfillment of prophecy. God's purposes will surely be accomplished.[16]

It is beyond the scope of the present brief chapter to include more than this cursory sampling of statements from this period. As the war ended and the nation moved into the reconstruction period of the late 1860s and the 1870s, Branson notes that quotations in the *Review and Herald* concerning national affairs seem to have been taken exclusively from well-known, radical Republican publications.[17] Ellen White criticized the government and the Christian churches for having given such meager help to educate and care for former slaves.[18] Clearly, the sympathies of church leaders were with the poor and oppressed.

Yet, the church still saw little hope in the prospects of changing societal structures. Concerning the last presidential election before his death, in 1880, James White wrote: "It should be our study to adapt ourselves, as far as possible without compromising truth, to all who come within the reach of our influence, and at the same time stand free from the strife and corruptions of the parties that are striving for the mastery."[19]

A new theme is introduced. Not only is seeking to reform society placing the emphasis in the wrong place because the culture is beyond redemption, but political activism, by taking partisan positions may alienate prospective converts and divide the church. Ellen White supported this theme, although she did give balance by lamenting the lack of involvement by the churches–including Adventists–in the social reconstruction and uplifting of the colored people following the war.[20]

In a definitive statement written in 1899, she called for Seventh-day Adventists to bury political questions, not to vote for political parties, and not to take part in political schemes for division may be brought into the church. Teachers in the church or schools who show zeal in politics should be relieved of their responsibilities. Our people are not called to engage in politics or become interested in political questions. In summary:

> It is a mistake for you to link your interests with any political party, to cast your vote with them or for them. Those who stand as educators, as ministers, as laborers together with God in any line have no battles to fight in the political world. Their citizenship is in heaven. The Lord calls upon them to stand as a separate and peculiar people. He would have no schisms in the body of believers.[21]

In the third quarter of the nineteenth century then, the Adventist church began to take note of the pressing public issues of the day and to speak to them with a political rhetoric. But this involvement was not for the purpose of creating a more just society or advancing the Kingdom of God on earth. It was rather to point out how far government had fallen from God's purpose for it and to announce its coming doom and the inauguration of the eschatological Kingdom that would make all things new. Thus Butler's designation of this period as *political apocalyptic*.

Religious Liberty and Temperance

By the 1880s, a gradual shift in the position of the church vis-a-vis government was taking place. In certain limited areas Adventists were beginning to engage in the political arena with the goal of influencing public policy. The two major areas of such activity were religious liberty and temperance.

The struggle for religious liberty could be justified in that it would make possible the preaching of the pure Gospel and thus allow more people to hear the message and prepare for the coming of Christ. Prohibition was a moral cause because liquor so dulled the minds of its slaves that they could not comprehend God's last message.

The church organized to oppose the National Reform Association which sought a religious amendment to the constitution and national Sunday laws. Sometimes perplexing situations arose such as bills to close saloons on Sunday. In California the Adventists allied with the League of Freedom (representing liquor dealers, saloons, and immigrants) to defeat pending Sunday legislation, but the church also campaigned, along with other conservative churches, for the banning of alcohol, an effort which eventually led to the prohibition amendment to the U. S. Constitution.

Adventists also helped to defeat the "Blair Bill" which prohibited many Sunday activities under the guise of protecting working people and which received support from many major denominations. Their activities in support of these goals included publications, organized voting, lectures, rallies, and sending representatives to present their position before congress.[22]

During this period another major breakthrough occurred. In 1882, an Adventist pastor, William C. Gage, was elected mayor of Battle Creek, Michigan–the first Adventist to run for and win public office. Even though temperance was a leading issue in the election, the event was so contrary to past Adventist practice that George Butler, then president of the General Conference, felt that it called for an explanation to the church. He wrote in part:

> It is well known that our people do not take as active a part in politics as some others. Some of them vote; some do not. But few of them vote unless they think they see some important moral principle involved in the issue, such as the question of slavery years ago or the question of temperance now. There is no question but that there is a feeling quite prevalent among us that it is not safe to dabble much in the pool of politics. . . .
>
> With the exception of the temperance question, we see very little in politics at the present time that should influence our people to participate in political excitement . . . the great moral issues of the present time are few and far between.
>
> Looking for the Lord Jesus, as we do, to put an end to all this prevailing corruption, how can we afford to mix in the political strife or bathe in the dirty pool of politics? We cannot do it. We consider it a dangerous thing for any of our people to hold civil office, and be brought into constant conflict with influences which surround public men.[23]

The door had been opened. While relatively few American Adventists have sought public office since then, some have, and those who have succeeded include congressional representatives and a governor. A number have also served in appointive rather than elective government positions. The church also retains a specialist at its Washington, DC, headquarters to serve as a liaison with the United States Congress in order to influence legislation. In some countries outside of the United States, it is common for Adventists to be involved in government–at least one even serving as a head of state.

The major point is, however, that Adventists who attain high office today are not an embarrassment to the church the way they were in the 1880s, nor do they call forth apologies. They are honored, written about, and invited to address church gatherings. Adventists have definitely become more comfortable with the political process.

> Encouraging Adventists toward the ballot box, petitions, temperance rallies and, on occasion, public office, Mrs. White typified the *political prophetic* that brought Seventh-day Adventism within the borders of the political process. The Adventists, as a prophetic people, were to use their voice to sustain the Republic as long as possible. The irony of their position, of course, involved them in a particular vocational hazard. They wished to delay the end in order to preach that the end was soon.[24]

The Twentieth Century

In this century Adventists have continued a cautious engagement in those public issues in which they have discerned moral content or which they have felt to be in their interests. Thus, they set up a War Service Commission during the second World War to secure noncombatant status and Sabbath rights for Adventist military personnel. General Conference president, J. L. McElhany, wrote a public letter of protest to Franklin D. Roosevelt over the appointment of Myron Taylor as personal representative to the Vatican. (Adventists would later protest the appointment of William Wilson by Ronald Reagan to the same position.) They joined with Protestants and Other Americans United for the Separation of Church and State to oppose Roman Catholic attempts to secure state funding for their parochial schools. They were active in opposing Sunday laws in the 1950s which eventually led to the Supreme Court decision of 1961 that Sunday laws are not religious in character and thus permissible. In this case the church had entered an *amicus curiae* brief stating that such laws violated the first amendment.[25]

Yet the political prophetic voice remained cautious and highly selective. A major theme remained that the calling of Adventists was to prepare people for the coming of the Lord, and that to involve themselves in public concerns would not only drain away energy from that task, but by taking sides would also alienate some who might otherwise be open to this message. For example, in 1928, an unsigned editorial–presumably by editor Francis M. Wilcox–discussed the problem in the light of the upcoming presidential election:

> God has commissioned His church with a special message to the world. It is the message

of Christ's soon coming, of the hour of God's judgment, of the necessary preparation of heart and life to stand in this solemn hour. The message is to all men of every class. We cannot array ourselves on one side or the other of the great divisions of society that exist in the world. By doing so we shall close the door of entrance to hearts which otherwise might be reached.[26]

It is sometimes difficult to determine on what basis issues have been viewed as having moral content and thus appropriate areas for church intervention. Why work for temperance but not for fair housing? Why oppose slavery but not racial discrimination? Why champion religious liberty but not equality for women? Syme hypothesizes:

> For the first time [Autumn Council of 1948] the Adventist church formulated an official position on church-state relations, stressing a belief in strict separatism. But in practice, the Adventist position remained separatist only to the point where a risk might develop to the church's control over its institutions.[27]

Perhaps the greatest modern challenge to Adventism's political self-identity came during the Civil Rights movement of the 1960s. Many of the church's minority leaders and members felt that it should take a more positive public stand for changes that they felt would bring about a more just society. Church leaders in general, however, opted for a low profile. After noting that many other churches were making pronouncements and clergymen were joining Freedom Marches, editor Nichol wrote:

> Such pronouncements and acts have been a part of the present over-all concept of many churchmen that one of the chief functions of the church is to reform the social order. This is known as the social gospel, and has increasingly marked our day, as personal evangelism to save men's souls has departed. Against the emphasis on the social gospel we, in common with all conservative religious groups, have consistently raised our voices, and rightly so.[28]

Later the same year, an associate editor amplified the position:

> Seventh-day Adventists are of the firm conviction that political questions not directly involving religion or matters of conscience are strictly out of bounds for churches and church agencies. The increasing tendency of the major religious bodies in the United States to take a public stand on strictly secular matters and to attempt to influence public policy with respect to them prostitutes their moral authority to affairs that Christ significantly omitted from the gospel commission. The apostles were instructed to teach and baptize, not to discuss politics or to lobby in congress, lest they blunt their witness to the truth of heaven by becoming involved in controversial matters of an earthly nature.[29]

Chapter 4

The historical development seems to have followed two streams. In the 1860s, church leaders were not hesitant to speak out. However, they did it not to bring about societal changes but to illustrate their apocalyptic of doom. By the 1960s, the church would either (1) not speak at all, lest it offend and divide or (2) speak with intention of bringing about change but limiting the issues to certain ones that seemed to be in the church's interests. The contrast between Adventism's relations to these two great crises in American history, approximately 100 years apart, has led some to conclude:

> In our early days as a movement we indeed appeared to affirm an eschatological other-worldliness that informed an altruistic this-worldliness. And this orientation found expression in such other-serving causes as abolition and reconstruction, causes that Ellen White and the pioneers knew full well would result in a greater sharing of the economic pie with the dispossessed. In our more recent days we appear to articulate an eschatological other-worldliness and to use the same as a rationale for not challenging those social structures which reward us with greater access to life chances.[30]

Perhaps a partial explanation for the shift from *political apocalyptic* to *political prophetic* can be found in the development of Adventism from a sect in high tension with society toward a denomination that has accommodated, at least somewhat, to its culture and enjoys social respectability. The denunciations of

James White, John Andrews, and Uriah Smith do not fit well with the public pronouncements of the church in the 1990s. Some have seen this illustrated in the history of the portrayal of the second beast of Revelation 13.

> Like sectarians [Adventists] retained their view of America as the two-horned beast of Revelation 13, but like the evangelicals, they permitted the contours of the beast to soften in the third phase of Adventist development. Pictorial illustrations in Adventist journals and books denote the iconographic metamorphosis. In the 1850s a Uriah Smith woodcut of the animal unveiled America as a hideous, boarlike beast with a long row of venomous teeth. In the 1870s and 1880s the beast gradually lost teeth, pictorially, until by 1905 it had become an affable American buffalo. S. N. Haskell, a prominent Adventist at the turn of the century, referred to the American beast as 'lamblike,' where for earlier interpreters it had possessed only lamblike horns. Within another generation, the onetime harsh woodcut gargoyle had mollified into the gamboling little lamb of 1940's Adventist evangelistic charts.[31]

Where does the church stand in the late twentieth century? No general repudiation of its historic positions of apocalyptic or withdrawal has taken place. Yet, subtle changes can be seen. On June 27, 1985, after consultation with the sixteen world vice presidents of the Seventh-day Adventist Church, President Neal C. Wilson issued a series of public statements expressing the church's position on peace, racism, home and family, and drugs. The documents urged "every nation to beat its 'swords into plowshares'" and proclaimed that the "Adventist hope must manifest and translate itself into deep concern for the well-being of every member of the human family." In a world of conflict, Adventists "desire to be known as peacemakers and work for worldwide justice and peace under Christ as the head of a new humanity." The church "deplores all forms of racism, including the political policy of apartheid with its enforced segregation and legalized discrimination."[32]

A few years later, President Wilson visited a peace conference in the then Soviet Union and made a public appeal to the Soviet government on behalf of human rights.[33] Activist articles are beginning to make their way into Adventist publications. As an example, the Andrews University school paper discussed the current South African situation and the relation of the Adventist church to apartheid.[34]

At the quinquenniel World Session of the General Conference of Seventh-day Adventists held in Indianapolis, Indiana, in July of 1990, further positions were set forth. Reporting on the developments, the *Adventist Review* stated:

> Responding to social issues frequently raised in the United States and overseas, General Conference leaders released the following statements during the fifty-fifth session of the church. Although these statements were not discussed or voted by the

session, they fairly represent the position of the church.

The statements that followed dealt with bans on selling assault weapons to civilians, pornography, an affirmation of family calling for renewal and healing, homelessness and poverty, stewardship of the environment (ecology), the Christian response to AIDS, and chemical use, abuse, and dependency.[35]

Times seem to be changing. The extent to which members have individually incorporated those changes or, in their thinking, are still part of the denomination of the 1960s, the 1920s, the 1880s, or even the 1860s may help to explain the differences in attitudes toward public issues among the membership. We must now inquire how this historical perspective can help us to understand the relationships between religion and politics among Seventh-day Adventists.

References

[1] Jonathan M. Butler, "Adventism and the American Experience," in *The Rise of Adventism*, ed. Edwin S. Gaustad, (New York: Harper & Row, 1974), 174.

[2] Ibid., 175-176.

[3] Ibid., 177.

[4] James White as quoted in a verbatim report of the discussions about church organization, *The Review and Herald*, 23 October, 1860, 178.

[5] John N. Andrews, "Thoughts on Revelation XIII and XIV," *Second Advent Review and Sabbath Herald*, 19, May, 1851, 81-86.

[6] See Charles Teel, Jr., "Withdrawing Sect, Accommodating Church, Prophesying Remnant: Dilemmas in the Institutionalization of Adventism," paper presented at the 1980 Theological Consultation for Seventh-day Adventist Administrators and Religion Scholars, 37-44.

[7] Roy Branson, "Ellen G. White—Racist or Champion of Equality?" *Review and Herald*, 9 April, 1970, 2-3.

[8] Ellen G. White, *Testimonies for the Church*, 9 vols. (Mountain View, CA: Pacific Press Publishing Assn., 1948), 1:359. Ellen White references in this paragraph were originally written in the late 1850s or early 1860s.

[9] Ibid., 1:202.

[10] Ibid., 1:254, 258.

[11] Ibid., 1:257.

[12] Editorial comment before "Letter to the President," *Review and Herald*, 23 September, 1862, 130.

[13] J. N. Andrews, "Slavery," *Review and Herald*, 25 October, 1864, 172.

[14]James White, "Thoughts on Revelation XIII," *Review and Herald*, 11 November, 1862, 188.

[15]Ellen G. White, *Spiritual Gifts: The Great Controversy between Christ and His Angels, and Satan and His Angels* (Battle Creek, MI: James White, 1858), 191-193.

[16]"Politics," *Review and Herald*, 11 September, 1856, 152.

[17]Roy Branson, "Slavery and Prophecy," *Review and Herald*, 16 April, 1970, 7-9.

[18]E. G. White, *Testimonies*, 9:205.

[19]James White, "The Political Campaign," *Review and Herald*, 11 March 1880, 176.

[20]E. G. White, *Testimonies*, 9:205.

[21]Ellen G. White, *Fundamentals of Christian Education* (Nashville, TN: Southern Publishing Assn., 1923), 475-486. Quotation from pp. 478-479.

[22]For a brief but detailed review of these activities, see Eric D. Syme, "A History of Adventist Views on Church and State Relations," *Spectrum*, 5, no. 3 (1973): 42-53.

[23]George I. Butler, "Politics and Temperance," *Review and Herald*, 11 April, 1882, 234.

[24]Jonathan Butler, 194.

[25]Syme, 5:42-53.

[26] "The Question of Politics," *The Advent Review and Sabbath Herald*, 19 January 1928, 10.

[27] Syme, 5:49.

[28] F. D. Nichol, "Unity in the Faith," *Review and Herald*, 29 April 1965, 12.

[29] R. F. Cottrell, "Churches Meddling in Politics." *Review and Herald*, 2 July 1965, 12.

[30] Teel, 44.

[31] Jonathan Butler, 191. For the story of the pictorial development of the two-horned beast from 1855 to 1947, including eight different pictures, see Ron Graybill, "America: The Magic Dragon," *Insight*, 30 November 1971, 6-12.

[32] "GC President Issues Statements on Racism, Peace, Home and Family, and Drugs, *Adventist Review*, 30 June 1985, 2-3.

[33] Neal C. Wilson, "Proposals for Peace and Understanding," *Spectrum* 19 (November 1988): 44-48.

[34] Craig van Rooyen, "Adventism vs. Apartheid–Are We Fighting?" *The Student Movement*, 18 October 1989, 8-9.

[35] Neal C. Wilson, "SDA Position Statements: GC Leaders Target Concerns for the Adventist Church, "*Adventist Review*, 26 July - 2 August 1990, 10-12.

Chapter 5

The Adventist Connection

Seeking a Framework

e have noted that a number of reasons exist for being able to predict attitudes toward public issues on the basis of various measures of religion among American Protestants–even though our predicting powers are far from perfect. We also have noted something of how the history of Seventh-day Adventism has shaped

its attitude toward government. Can we now put the two together and find some sort of framework by which we can understand the connection between religion and politics among Adventists? Doubtless, a number of such frameworks could be constructed. One recent attempt that might prove helpful has been offered by Malcolm Bull and Keith Lockhart.[1]

In brief, Bull and Lockhart hold that America, in its national infancy, took the position of the "promised land," the new millennial kingdom. Adventism rejected this claim and offered a spiritual alternative–itself. The authors draw the picture in broad strokes at the outset:

> In their formative years, the Seventh-day Adventists rejected the essentials of the American myth. They did not accept that the republican experiment would lead to the betterment of humanity or that it would be a lasting success. They consigned America to eventual destruction, and in place of the nation, they daringly substituted themselves as the true vehicle for the redemption of the world. America had offered sanctuary to generations of immigrants from Europe; Adventism sought to provide a sanctuary from America. By presenting itself as an alternative to the Republic in this way, the church rapidly came to operate as an alternative to America in the social sphere as well, as Adventists replicated the institutions and functions of American society.[2]

American Civil Religion

In order to follow this line of reasoning some background is desirable. How could a *religious body* be set against a *nation?* Isn't that like comparing oranges and apples? The answer lies in the concept of *civil religion* which

> refers to the view of some people that the foundation of their society and the events that mark its progress through history are parts of a larger, divine scheme of things; the political structure and the political acts that flow out of that structure have a transcendental dimension–God is at work in our nation, and as such we have a destiny.[3]

While civil religion does not endorse any particular denomination–and not even Christianity as such–it employs a broader set of shared religious symbols that transcend partisan religious differences. Thus, we have almost a "second national anthem" in "God Bless America," our coins proclaim "In God We Trust," and the phrase "Under God" is included in our pledge of allegiance. Nearly all presidents, especially in inaugural addresses, have spoken of America as having a divinely ordained mission to fulfill in bringing about God's will for humankind. Civil religion has its "holy days" (Fourth of July, Memorial Day, Veterans Day, etc.) and its martyrs (Lincoln, Kennedy, King, etc.).[4]

Bull points out that "civil religion has proved easier to characterize in the eighteenth and nineteenth centuries than in the twentieth. The American Revolution and the formation of the Republic were viewed in unambiguously religious terms."[5] In the struggle against Britain, the foe was pictured as the antichrist while America was the persecuted woman of Revelation 12. Victory would herald the dawn of the millennium. As we noted in chapter 2, mainline Protestantism–then evangelical–largely endorsed postmillennialism. By the influence of the Gospel, society would be perfected and a temporal kingdom would be established. It was a time of great optimism. This civil millennialism "was communicated to every level of society in order to effect the requisite moral transformation. The millennium would arrive only if the discourse of civil religion achieved a monopoly."[6]

William Miller, with his predictions of an approaching catastrophic end to this planet, challenged this monopoly of orthodoxy. And when the prophesied disaster did not occur at the predicted time, a nucleus of the Millerites clung to the correctness of the time but shifted the event to Christ's coming to the second apartment of the sanctuary in heaven to begin a work of investigative judgment. At the conclusion of this investigation, Christ would return to destroy the wicked and save the saints. In the meantime, His people should employ their energies in preparing for this climactic event. Out of this nucleus grew the Seventh-day Adventists Church.

Heretical Alternative

Bull takes pains to differentiate between *heresy* and *apostasy*. Heresy does not repudiate orthodoxy as apostasy does; it merely reinterprets it. "Heresy employs the same language as orthodoxy but attempts to order its discourse to some other end."[7] Adventists, then, became heretics of American civil religion by employing concepts and language used to describe the nation but reinterpreting them to describe their own mission.

For example, civil religionists used the framework of Christian eschatology to describe America as a special nation, chosen by God to bring about the millennial kingdom. But

> if through the example of America, the world was brought to perfection, there would be no need for divine intervention in human history. The American dream threatened to undermine the Adventist hope. To retain hope, the Adventists transformed that dream into a nightmare, seeking out contemporary evidence of American hypocrisy.[8]

Thus, as noted in chapter 4, America becomes the persecuting beast, and Adventism is the latter-day descendent of the woman in the wilderness.

Another example is the Sabbath. For Adventists, the seventh-day Sabbath is not merely a day of rest but a sign of loyalty to God against the apostasy of the world in the closing conflict of the great controversy between Christ and Satan.

> The Sunday Sabbath was central to the ideology of civil religion. . . . Disregard for Sunday was one of the obstacles to the realization of the millennium that the revivalists had sought to overcome; it was one of the issues on which Beecher thought the future of the West would

hinge. The Adventists were Sabbatarians all right, but theirs was an alternative Sabbath that enshrined the deviant form of millennialism they had inherited from the Millerites.[9]

It is important to note that Bull does not use the term *heresy* in a pejorative fashion–the way we are usually inclined to view it–or in an evaluative manner at all. It simply represents an alternative interpretation of reality to that held by orthodoxy. Neither is orthodoxy evaluated in terms of true or false. It is an ideology that has come to be widely accepted and institutionalized in the practices of the society–in this case, the ideology of civil religion.

Alternative Institutions

But Adventists did not simply offer opposing belief systems to civil religion. They also created structures similar to those by which orthodoxy sought to extend its sphere of control. "Having defined itself over against civil religion, Adventism needed to develop a parallel set of institutions in order to maintain its identity and to compete with the progress of its rival."[10]

Thus, over against the movement for universal education which would foster common ideals and promote the American Dream, Adventists established their own school system. Civil religionists were interested in perfecting society through temperance and other reforms. "Adventists adopted health reform, not in order to improve the body in preparation for an earthly millennium, but to achieve a perfect control of the appetite in readiness for translation."[11] The formation of the Medical Cadet Corps allowed the church to create its own form of military service without undesirable influence from the state.[12]

Especially intriguing is the explanation of an alternative to the American democratic system in its organizational structures. Adventism rejected the individualism upon which that system was based and preferred a hierarchical administrative and economic system. The hierarchy seems to be based on the visions of Ellen White of the heavenly realm where a monarchy prevails. Such organization might be expected of a group who believed that the American experiment would fail and be superseded by divine government.[13]

So with missions and evangelism. About the time that America was seeing itself as being responsible for heralding the American Dream and "making the world safe for democracy," Seventh-day Adventists were engaging on a global missionary program.

> Countries within the American sphere of influence proved particularly receptive to the Adventist message. Interestingly, it is through American power that Adventist eschatology becomes credible. In operating as the world's policeman, the United States rehearses the very role that Adventists expect it to play in enforcing the universal Sunday law.[14]

Many other parallels could be cited from Bull and Lockhart, but these examples suffice to illustrate the theme. The elaborate Adventist society can be perceived here as "an attempt to insulate the church from the flawed Republic and to provide alternative institutions that would (unlike American institutions) bring about the millennium."[15]

> This imitation of civil religion has resulted in the development of a vast network of institutions that mirrors those provided by the American state. In consequence, it is possible for a twentieth-century Adventist to spend his entire life within the Adventist subculture. He or she can be educated from nursery to graduate school entirely by Adventist teachers, receive medical attention only from Adventist doctors, work only for denominational institutions or businesses, travel all over the world as a guest of Adventist missions, retire to one of the church's rest homes, and expect to die in the Adventist hospital in which he or she was born.[16]
>
> Adventism has recreated America within America. It has turned the ideology of civil religion inside out to form a faith that consigns the nation to damnation and locates salvation within another social group.[17]

Implications of the Adventist Alternative

The reader may feel that the argument of Bull and Lockhart is flawed in a number of respects and in this judgment may be correct. Ross, for example, points out that the authors have failed to balance the positive Adventist stress on being good citizens, based on passages like Romans 13, with the negative emphasis of

Adventist eschatology. He also denies that the Adventist ominous view of the future conflict calls forth "a constant apocalyptic commentary on contemporary events."[18]

Yet, even if we grant that Bull and Lockhart pushed their theory to the extreme and were highly selective in their choice of illustrative material, some such framework as they present seems to fit the experience of the Adventist church. The historical perspective of Adventism viewed in chapter 4 can be integrated into such a theory.

If this much be conceded, how would such a framework help us to understand the connection between the religion and the political stance of Adventists? For one thing, we could understand the Adventist entry into the public arena on behalf of religious liberty and its emphasis on the second of Lovin's basic claims of religion–to guarantee freedom. "The general effort to keep church and state within defined boundaries can be seen as a by-product of the belief that America would one day establish the universal Sunday law and persecute Sabbath keepers."[19]

Such a connection leads Adventists to espouse such causes as freedom of speech, religion, and the press and to oppose government involvement in religion such as authorized prayer in public schools, aid for parochial education, and diplomatic relations with churches. Such are liberal positions, but Adventists uphold them even though they would be more comfortable theologically with evangelicals than with the liberal coalition that joins them in this crusade.

On the other hand, Adventists have enjoyed a relatively amicable relationship with the state, given their belief in the Biblical doctrine of divinely ordained government. Bull and Lockhart suggest that the "source of this amity is Adventism's willingness to keep hostility in the realm of theology and to express its uncertainties about the state by replicating, rather then [sic] attacking, national institutions."[20]

Given these alternative structures, we might expect Adventism to uphold the capitalist form of government against militant, atheistic communism and to defend the status quo which has preserved traditional values. In other words, Adventists ought to be for *order* (conservative) except where it threatens *freedom* (liberal). On the other hand, since it presents an alternative system rather than seeking to perfect societal institutions as civil religion does, Adventism may have much less concern with the liberal cause of seeking for new forms of social *justice*. Their eschatological scenario tends to lead Adventists to place their hope in the destruction of society (and the creation of a new world order) rather than in its improvement. Adventist theology tends to see the root of the world's problems in sin in the individual heart rather than in sinful societal structures.

But we have been speaking of Adventists as if they were a uniform political entity when our thesis from the beginning has been that individuals vary on their politics according to certain measures of religion and background variables such as ethnicity. Bull and Lockhart recognized that Adventism is politically fluid in many ways and suggested that some Adventists are now more willing to engage society in a positive manner and relinquish their separatism. They felt that these new activists were led by doctors–starting with John Harvey Kellogg–and educators.[21]

Given all of the material in this chapter and the first four, our task is to predict ways in which differences in religious beliefs, behaviors, and experiences among Adventists may relate to their positions on public issues.

Making the Connection

The theoretical framework we have been constructing would lead us to predict that Adventists most committed to the traditions of the church are most likely to resist any government intrusion into religion, while at the same time adopting many elements of the American system in their beliefs and practices. More specifically, those Adventists who believe strongly in the historic interpretation of the second beast of Revelation 13 as representing the United States would be more likely to take such a stance than those who were more tentative about the prophecy.

Unfortunately, we do not have data on varying prophetic interpretations in our sample. We do, however, have responses on the extent to which subjects agree with certain key Adventist doctrines–including whether Adventism is the true remnant church and the inspiration of Ellen White, who supported the historic interpretation. We expect, then, that those scoring highest on the Adventist orthodoxy scale are the most likely either to withdraw from political concerns completely or to favor separation-of-church-and-state issues and preservation of the status quo in government since any change (such as an amendment to the Constitution) could bring about the long-awaited persecution.

Chapter 5

In addition to actual ideological content, we must also consider the conservative manner of thinking. Seventh-day Adventism arose in the mid-nineteenth century. Its doctrinal foundations were laid by its pioneers, and its ethics were shaped by Victorian morality. Therefore, those Adventists who most strongly adhere to Adventist orthodoxy should also be the most conservative in the political arena, basically favoring the status quo, for they place high worth on heritage from the past. That which was important at the beginning of a great movement retains its importance over the years.

Adventists have traditionally interpreted the meaning of sickness, tragedy, and death as the result of a dualism in the universe, revealing the presence of a powerful evil personage. A favorite theme of Ellen White was the great controversy between Christ and Satan stretching from paradise lost to paradise restored. Those Adventists most orthodox likely tend to oppose forces that seem to be part of the conspiracy of evil, such as atheistic communism, political Catholicism, and secular humanism. The latter is manifested by its attempts to undermine family and societal values which reflect Christian principles.

The more orthodox Adventists are also likely to view these sinister forces as having infiltrated liberal Christianity through the influence of evolutionary teachings, through Biblical criticism, and through denial of the obligation to obey the ten commandments. Since liberal churches have long been identified with the social gospel, including political action for civil rights and social justice causes, orthodox Adventists are more likely to reject such action as tainted and tending to undermine the genuine Gospel.

Adventists who tend to see their religion in terms of individual sin and individual salvation are not as likely to favor churches becoming involved in social action to improve the lot of the less fortunate. For these believers, the Christian message betters society by changing hearts–one by one. Related to this is the so-called "Protestant ethic" which encourages believers to work hard and not waste money on frivolous pleasures. The resulting prosperity and upward mobility may come to be regarded as a sign of divine favor, and the position of those less fortunate can be construed as their just desserts. Thus Adventists with a more individualistic world view of religion might be expected to repudiate much of the liberal agenda and espouse much (but not all) of the conservative one.

This group is likely to include those who expect a swift and catastrophic end to the world by the Second Advent of Christ and those whose understanding of sin and its solution is cast more in individualistic than in communal terms. It also may take in, however, those high on the experiential dimension of religion; that is, those whose religion is characterized by a heightened sense of divine presence and an awareness of having experienced personal conversion. While this dimension is not necessarily incompatible with social action, pietism and mysticism have long been associated with the privatization of religion.

Since religious belief and religious practice are related, especially among conservatives, those Adventists who attend church more regularly, who participate more fully in church functions, who are more committed to the church as an institution, and who engage more often in devotional practices recommended by the church are likely to exhibit the same behaviors described above as those with strong orthodox beliefs. In all of this, however, we must keep in mind that the dynamics within ethnic minorities are likely to differ substantially due to their particular experience in American history and their present status in society.

On the other hand, those who are less orthodox are likely to possess a mind set more willing to experiment with political and economic changes as possible solutions to societal problems, tend to be more optimistic about the prospects of making structural improvements in society, and thus are more likely to employ social and political action and to work for social justice than are their more orthodox fellow believers.

Adventists whose religious orientation tends to be open and tentative rather than fixed and dogmatic–whether the content of their beliefs is conservative or liberal–are more likely to favor liberal political positions. They are be especially likely to minimize the religious function of *order* and oppose legislation of morality for they realize that their positions–however important to them personally–may be viewed differently by other sincere and reasonable people. Thus, they are likely to emphasize the religious function of championing *freedom*. They tend to have an "I disagree with what you say, but I will fight for your right to say it" mentality.

No doubt, the most-employed construct for how people are religious is the intrinsic-extrinsic orientations developed by Gordon Allport[22] as an outgrowth of his definition of mature religiosity.[23] While extrinsic or immature religion is largely instrumental, intrinsic or mature religion is a master motive that leads its possessor in service to his or her faith and the world. It encompasses tolerance and understanding. Therefore, Adventists higher on intrinsic or mature measures might be expected to be more interested in the plight of the less fortunate and less rigidly nationalistic than extrinsic or immature members.

Finally, according to Greeley, how one conceives of God helps to determine one's attitudes toward public issues, especially those dealing with social problems.[24] Adventists whose images of God are the "softer" ones of mother, spouse, lover, and friend might be expected to be more supportive of a liberal social agenda and of "peace politics" than those who are more likely to envision God with the sterner attributes of father, master, judge, and king.

Given the logical connections between conservative-liberal religion and conservative-liberal politics and given the historical perspective on Protestantism in general and Seventh-day Adventism in particular, which we have reviewed, the above expectations seem certainly reasonable. Whether or not this reasonableness is supported by fact, however, is an empirical question. To determine the answer, we now turn to the information that we have collected from a national sample of American Seventh-day Adventists.

References

[1]Malcolm Bull and Keith Lockhart, *Seeking a Sanctuary: Seventh-day Adventism and the American Dream* (New York: Harper & Row, 1989), hereinafter cited as *Sanctuary*; Malcolm Bull, "The Seventh-day Adventists: Heretics of

Chapter 5

American Civil Religion," *Sociological Analysis* 50 no. 2 (1989): 177-187, hereinafter cited as "Heretics."

²*Sanctuary*, ix-x.

³Ronald L. Johnstone, *Religion in Society: A Sociology of Religion*, 3rd ed. (Englewood Cliffs, NJ: Prentice Hall, 1988), 134.

⁴Ibid., 134-137.

⁵"Heretics," 179.

⁶Ibid., 180.

⁷Ibid., 178.

⁸*Sanctuary*, 48.

⁹"Heretics," 183.

¹⁰Ibid., 184.

¹¹Ibid.

¹²*Sanctuary*, 144.

¹³Ibid., 109-110.

¹⁴Ibid., 168.

¹⁵Ibid., 109.

¹⁶"Heretics," 184-185.

[17]*Sanctuary*, 171.

[18]Gary M. Ross, "The Politics of Liberty," *Adventist Review*, 8 March 1990, 15.

[19]*Sanctuary*, 149.

[20]Ibid., 170.

[21]See *Sanctuary*, 218-243.

[22]Gordon W. Allport, "The Religious Context of Prejudice," *Journal for the Scientific Study of Religion* 5 (Fall 1966): 447-457.

[23]Gordon W. Allport, *The Individual and His Religion* (New York: Macmillan, 1950).

[24]Andrew M. Greeley, "Religious Imagery as a Predictor Variable in the General Social Survey," paper presented to the Society for the Scientific Study of Religion, Chicago, October 1984.

Chapter 6

The Religion of American Adventists

In a search for the way religion and politics are related among Seventh-day Adventists, we surveyed 419 adult members, randomly selected from Adventist households in the United States.[1] Our questionnaire collected three basic types of information: religious attitudes and behaviors, political attitudes and behaviors, and personal information. In this chapter we consider the findings on the religion variables. How religious are American Adventists? Or, to put it another way, How are American Adventists religious? In subsequent chapters we examine the other two types of data and the relationships among all three of the basic types.

For more than thirty years researchers have been suggesting that religion is a multidimensional variable; that is, one can be religious in a variety of ways. An early statement by Charles Glock proposed five dimensions: ideological (belief), intellectual (information), ritualistic (religious behaviors), experiential (emotions), and consequential (life effects).[2] Later researchers have found ways to divide and reclassify and thus to arrive at as many as eleven dimensions.[3]

For our study we chose a number of religious dimensions: belief or orthodoxy, religious experience, church-related behaviors, devotional practice, salience or importance of religion, foundational world view, intrinsic-extrinsic orientation, religious maturity, and image of God. All but one of these (salience) are measured by several items. Here is how American Adventists rate on these dimensions.

Orthodoxy

Orthodoxy or belief is an ideological measure designed to see how Adventists might differ on doctrines which are historically important to the church but which have become more or less controversial in recent years. Only items that refer to distinctive Adventist doctrines were included. Thus, items concerning the existence of God, the divinity of Jesus, and the reality of the devil—measures of orthodoxy on most surveys of the general Christian population—were omitted as we assumed that they would have little variance in this group.

The Belief Scale consists of six questions. The sample subjects responded to each doctrinal statement on a scale of 1 to 5, where 1 indicated "strongly disagree" and 5 indicated "strongly agree." For ease of interpretation we combined responses 1 and 2 into a "disagree" category and 4 and 5 into an "agree" category. The extent to which these two percentages fail to add to 100 percent equals the middle or "uncertain" choice.[4] The actual wording of the questionnaire is used.

ITEM	DISAGREE	AGREE
God created the world in six literal days, approximately 6000 years ago.	4%	91%
A person's standing before God is based on his/her obedience to God's law	25%	65%
The investigative judgment began in the second apartment of the heavenly sanctuary on October 22, 1844.	7%	78%
Jesus Christ will come the second time in our generation	5%	62%
The Seventh-day Adventist Church is God's true church.	8%	83%
Ellen White was inspired by God, and her writings are an authoritative guide for Adventists today.	5%	86%

Chapter 6

Substantial majorities agreed–and in all but two cases (law and Second Advent) strongly agreed–with these statements. Support for literal creation, true church, and Ellen White remains strong among these lay members despite the challenges of recent years. Even the hotly contested investigative judgment was supported by over three-fourths of the membership, although here the uncertain category rose to 15 percent. Still, only small minorities disagreed with any of these traditional statements.

The strong support for most Adventist doctrines does not invalidate, however, our basic assumption that Adventists do not all have the same religion for several reasons. (1) Religion involves much more than simply doctrinal agreement. (2) Even on the Orthodoxy Scale the range of score is sufficient for significant correlations. (3) Several doctrines were not as strongly supported.

The most surprising finding from the standpoint of historical Adventism is that only 62 percent agreed that Jesus Christ will come the second time in our generation. While few disagreed, a third were uncertain. One suspects that the hesitancy is not over the *fact* of His second coming but over its *imminence*. The long years of waiting and the often-repeated misreading of the "signs of the times" have taken their toll.

The most disturbing finding, however, ought to be the response to the "law" item. When these six statements were combined into a Belief Scale, the reliability (a measure of the consistency of the responses to the individual items) was found to be unacceptably low for a scale. The problem proved to be the question, "A person's standing before God is based on his/her obedience to God's law." Since this item is contrary to

Adventist teaching on righteousness by faith and represents a "works" righteousness, scoring was reversed so that *disagreement* placed one high on the Belief Scale. A glance at the above chart, however, reveals that the majority (65%) *agreed* with the statement, and about half (51%) *strongly agreed.* And those who agreed with the other items tended to agree most with this one. It was decided, therefore, to remove this item from the scale and treat it separately. The Belief Scale used in later analyses, then, contains the remaining five items and has a strong reliability or consistency.

The pattern of responses to the "law" item suggests two important implications: First, American Adventists, more than a hundred years after the Minneapolis Conference of 1888, are still not clear on righteousness by faith and tend to be "works" oriented. Second, those members who are most orthodox on historical doctrines like creation, investigative judgment, second advent, true church, and Ellen White are the ones most likely to depend on their law keeping to provide them with favorable standing in God's sight. Both of these implications should alarm church leaders.

Religious Experience

In contrast to the cognitive processes of belief, religious experience represents the feeling or emotional level. It refers to things like sensation of the divine presence, assurance of sins forgiven, and renewal through the new birth. While prophets, pentecostals, and mystics are particularly high on the experiential dimension, most believers experience religious emotions to some extent. Even within Adventism some congregations incorporate "feeling" into their worship services more than others do, and certain evangelists are more likely than others to rely on emotional appeals.

We included three questions to measure this dimension. They were adapted from those widely used in the literature on religious research with slight changes to fit the Adventist situation. The display follows the same format as that for orthodoxy.

ITEM	DISAGREE	AGREE
I frequently feel very close to God in prayer, during public worship, or at important moments in my daily life.	2%	89%
I often experience the joy and peace which comes from knowing my sins have been forgiven.	3%	89%
I am certain that I have had a conversion or born-again experience.	4%	83%

The high rate of agreement with these items indicates that American Adventists incorporate a great deal of subjective emotional experience into their religion. Or, at the very least, it says that they believe they *should* experience religion this way and answered accordingly. The responses to the three items are consistent among themselves, producing a strong reliability for the Experiential Scale.

Church-Related Behaviors

One of the oldest ways of determining religious commitment is to look at practices that support the church body–things like frequency of attendance and financial contributions. Here we move from the cognitive realm of belief and the affective realm of experience to the behavioral realm of action. "By their fruit you will recognize them" (Matt. 7:20 NIV).

We used four items to measure this dimension: church attendance, church involvement, witnessing activities, and financial giving. Here is how American Adventists scored on each.

The first question was: "If not prevented by unavoidable circumstances, how often do you attend church?" The responses were:

Rarely or never	9%
Once every month or two	5%
Two or three times a month	11%
At least once a week	75%

Three-fourths of the members claimed to be regular church attenders. The next question asked: "Do you hold an office or other service position in your local congregation?"

No	43%
Yes	57%

Over half were involved in internal or congregational-maintenance ministries. Obviously, this is related to the frequency of attendance.[5] The third question in the set inquired: "How active have you been this last year in outreach or witnessing activities?"

Rarely or never	40%
At least six times a year	14%
At least once a month	20%
At least once a week	26%

The subjects could define for themselves what would qualify as "outreach or witnessing activities." Presumably, they may have had in mind anything from giving Bible studies and conducting Revelation Seminars to leaving tracts in public rest rooms. Even with the loosest of definitions, however, witnessing activity fell way off compared with attendance and congregational service. Two-fifths did nothing, and less than half could be said to live any kind of witnessing life style.

The final item deals with financial support: "Last year, approximately what percentage of your gross income was contributed to the church or other religious causes?"

Less than 5%	18%
5% to 9%	11%
10% to 14%	41%
15% to 19%	15%
20% or more	15%

Treasurers on both local and conference levels, no doubt, will be surprised to learn that over 70 percent of the membership were contributing a minimum of 10 percent of their income. Studies of financial records (not individual questionnaires) usually suggest a lower figure. The discrepancy might be accounted for by the fact that active church members were more likely to return the survey instrument and thus the study is biased to some unknown degree in favor of more faithful members. Or a tendency may exist for members to answer with what they know they should have done rather than with what they actually did.

Devotional Practices

The Devotional Scale measures those religious behaviors which would be performed in a private or home setting rather than at public worship, such as private prayer, Bible study, reading religious literature, and participating in family worship. The question asked how often the respondent did each of the four behaviors.

Pray privately	Seldom or never	3%
	Less than weekly	6%
	At least weekly	13%
	Daily	78%
Study the Bible	Seldom or never	7%
	Less than weekly	15%
	At least weekly	34%
	Daily	44%

Read religious literature	Seldom or never	5%
	Less than weekly	15%
	At least weekly	50%
	Daily	30%
Participate in family worship	Seldom or never	28%
	Less than weekly	17%
	At least weekly	21%
	Daily	34%

With good consistency in the scale, the reliability is high. Note that 80 percent or more claimed to engage in the first three practices on at least a weekly basis, although fewer than half studied the Bible or read other religious literature daily. Family worship did not fare as well, with only a third of the homes having it every day and another 21 percent at least weekly, probably on Sabbath.

Salience

We included a one-item measure of the importance of religion to the person involved. It is a common question to many social surveys of religion–usually labeled "salience." The exact wording was: "All in all, how important would you say your religious faith is to you?"

Fairly unimportant	2%
Not too important	1%
Fairly important	3%
Quite important	18%
Extremely important	76%

Over three-fourths reported that their religious faith is extremely important to them with another 18 percent saying "quite important." Only a small number considered their religion as relatively unimportant. American Adventists take their faith quite seriously. Of course, some tendency to give the "right" answer may be operating.

Foundational World View

This dimension, Foundational World View, was drawn from some interesting work by researchers studying other groups. Based on Yinger's concept that how a person is religious is a more fundamental measure than how religious he or she is,[6] Benson and Williams asked their respondents to name the most basic human problem, the principal pathway to overcoming that problem, and the most important outcome of that "salvation."[7] They then connected these three components to determine if the respondent was agentic (individualistic) or communal in world view. Leege and Welch refined this measure in their study of Catholic parishioners.[8] We used a forced-choice form of the Leege and Welch model as a three-item Foundational World View measure, scored as one item and slightly modified to fit Adventist theology.

Our first question was: "Religion always identifies a basic human problem, something that is wrong with humans and their world. Indicate the *single* most basic problem." Choices were: "something lacking in my individual life," "separation of humans from God;

sinfulness," "lack of human community or closeness between people," or a write-in answer.

The second question was: "Religion always describes a path to salvation, a way that basic human problems can be overcome. Which of the following comes closest to that path?" Choices were: "doing good works to earn God's favor," "trusting in God's free gift of forgiveness," "working hard to make society better and more just," or a write-in answer.

The third item was: "Finally, religion talks about the outcomes of salvation. What is the most important outcome?" Choices were: "life on earth is changed; feel fulfillment, meaning," "live forever with God after the resurrection," "world changed so people live in peace and harmony," or a write-in answer.

Thus subjects could choose a given response or provide one of their own. Each response was labeled agentic (also individualistic) or communal (also communitarian). "Agentic religiosity focuses exclusively on an individual's problems, needs, and the religious solutions to them. Communal religiosity, however, focuses on those needs and problems that are commonly shared by all people and involve their relationships with each other."[9]

If an individual selected an agentic response to all three questions, the overall World View was coded as "individualistic." If a communal response was given to all three items, the World View was coded as "communitarian." Failure to be consistent earned a "mixed" coding. Only 1 percent of the sample were identified as communitarian; not surprising, given Adventist other-worldly theology. Most Adventists (78%)

seemed to be individualistic with about a fifth (21%) being mixed.

Intrinsic-Extrinsic Motivation

This motivation measure taps into the vast volume of work done on intrinsic-extrinsic orientations to religion, beginning with the seminal concepts of Gordon Allport.[10] It is one of the most-researched areas in the psychology of religion. Basically, those with extrinsic orientation use their religion as a *means* to gain some other goal–social approval, comfort in sorrow, even eternal salvation. In contrast, those who are intrinsically oriented see their religion as an *end* in itself. It is the master motive which controls all their actions. Such people give themselves to serve their God and their fellow humans without asking what they will get back.

In the questionnaire, ten items tap this concept. A number of instruments have been offered over the years to measure these orientations. Usually, they contain both intrinsic and extrinsic scales. We chose to use a brief single scale developed by Dean Hoge of Catholic University that uses those ten items that yielded the highest validity, reliability, item-to-item correlations, and item-to-scale correlations in his review.[11] We incorporated it into our instrument with permission from Dr. Hoge. The first seven items are intrinsic; the last three are extrinsic and are reversed-scored. Thus a high score on the scale indicates intrinsic orientation; a low score, extrinsic. The reliability is the highest of any of the scales.

Sample intrinsic items are: "My faith involves all of my life" and "Nothing is as important to me as serving God as best I know how." A sample extrinsic item is: "Although I am a religious person, I refuse to let religious considerations influence my everyday affairs." Most Adventists agreed with the intrinsic and disagreed with the extrinsic items. Of course, the respondents did not know which questions were part of which scale or even that scales were involved. In an effort to minimize response bias, no intrinsic/extrinsic labelling was done throughout the questionnaire.

With ten items, each having responses ranging from 1 to 5, the scale had a possible range of 10 to 50. And, indeed, the actual range was the same, although only one person scored 10, and 94 people scored 50. Actually, 97 percent were above the middle score of 30, 80 percent were above 40, 58 percent were above 45, and 22 percent scored the maximum of 50. If they responded honestly, American Adventists are very intrinsically oriented.

Religious Maturity

The religious maturity measure also stems from the pioneer work of Gordon Allport on orientation to religion. He identified the characteristics of a mature personality from a psychological standpoint and then attempted to apply them to the way a person is religious. Mature religion is "(1) well differentiated; (2) dynamic in character in spite of its derivative nature; (3) productive of a consistent morality; (4) comprehensive; (5) integral; and (6) fundamentally heuristic."[12] At the same time that it provides direction to life as a "master motive," it is flexible and responsive to new information, neither fanatic nor compulsive. It deals openly and honestly with "matters central to all existence," including the difficult questions of ethical responsibility and evil. It produces the ability to "act wholeheartedly even without absolute certainty. It can be sure without being cocksure."[13]

The questionnaire included an eleven-item Religious Maturity Scale developed by Roger Dudley and Robert Cruise.[14] The scale proved to have a lower reliability with this sample than desired, however. After inspection of the item analysis, the three items that correlated the poorest with the overall scale were dropped, leaving an eight-item scale for the analyses with an improved, but still moderate, reliability.

Measurement of the construct is difficult for it requires the respondent–in line with Allport's concept–to hold in tension wholehearted commitment to one's faith with flexibility and openness to new light and truth. Sample statements are: "My religious beliefs provide me with satisfying answers at this stage of my development, but I am prepared to alter them as new information becomes available." "While we can never be quite sure that what we believe is absolutely true, it is worth acting on the probability that it may be."

Individuals are asked to agree or disagree with statements that present what may seem to be opposing ideas. This is difficult for persons with rigid or dogmatic mind sets. Thus consistency on this scale is lower than on the others which have items that are more straightforward. Religious maturity, under this formulation, requires a mixture of humility, openness, and commitment.

Chapter 6

The mature faith is also comprehensive. It attempts to integrate all of life into its scheme of understanding. Thus a sample item is: "I have struggled in trying to understand the problems of evil, suffering, and death that mark this world." Such faith is dynamic, never stagnant. It is always growing, always journeying, but never, in this life, reaching the end of the journey.

The majority of Adventists agreed with the positive statements although the extent of agreement was not nearly as great as with belief, experiential, or intrinsic items. A slight slippage occurred with the statement: "I have found many religious questions to be difficult and complex so I am hesitant to be dogmatic or final in my assertions," where not quite the majority (48%) agreed that they are hesitant to be dogmatic or final. The biggest reversal, though, was on the negative item: "I could not commit myself to a religion unless I was certain that it is completely true." Here 88 percent agreed (71% strongly), although it is *disagreement* which scores high on the Religious Maturity Scale for it allows for further light and growth. It is not our purpose here to explore the ramifications of such dogmatism, but it should prove a fruitful field for further investigation and writing. Obviously, the direction of the responses to this question prevents the reliability from being better and limits the predictive power of the scale. Similar trends can be seen in the items that were dropped.

With eight items, each having responses ranging from 1 to 5, the combined scale had a possible range of 8 to 40. The actual range was the same and much more balanced than the Intrinsic Scale with just two people scoring at both 8 and 40. Only 64 percent were above the middle score of 24, only 15 percent were above 32, and less than 2 percent scored above 36. American Adventists are definitely not as advanced in religious maturity–as defined by this particular construct–as they are in orthodoxy, religious experience, and intrinsic motivation.

Religious Imagery

Andrew Greeley proposed that one's mental images of God are particularly important in determining social behaviors. How one conceives of God, Greeley felt, helps to determine one's attitudes toward public issues, especially those dealing with social problems. As mentioned in chapter 1, people whose images of God are the "softer" ones of mother, spouse, lover, and friend might be expected to be more supportive of a liberal social agenda and of "peace politics" than those who are more likely to describe God with the "sterner" figures of father, master, judge, and king. Greeley called this the "Grace Factor."[15]

We included the Grace Scale in our questionnaire. It lists four items, each containing two contrasting images: Mother-Father, Master-Spouse, Judge-Lover, and Friend-King. Respondents were asked: "On a scale of 1 to 7 where would you place your picture of God in each set?"

Respondents in this study were far more likely to go to the Father extreme than the Mother extreme (53% to 4%) on the first continuum but were more balanced on the last three (Master–29%, Spouse–19%; Judge–17%, Lover–22%; Friend–18%, King–31%). In all cases the midpoint (choice 4) was high (25%, 30%, 40%, and 35%, respectively). For the combined scale, the full range of 4 (21 people) to 28 (1 person) was realized. More people scored at 16 (33%), the midpoint, than at any other score, and only 16 percent were above that theoretical average. American Adventists appear to lean toward the sterner images of God.

Unfortunately, the scale proved to have almost no reliability at all in this sample and, therefore, was not used in the correlational analyses. A smaller scale, using only the two middle sets (Master-Spouse, Judge-Lover), was found to have adequate reliability and was used in some of later statistical calculations.

Unofficial Journals

A number of journals are circulated in the United States that are published by Adventist members but not officially sponsored by the church. Since these occupy various places on a conservative-moderate religious continuum, we decided to include several to see if valuing them was related to positions on public issues. Of course, this inclusion does not represent a dimension of religion as do the other measures presented, but affinity toward certain journals might provide some insight into one's religious values.

After an examination of perhaps a dozen candidates, four were selected. The criteria were that they should represent different–even extreme–postures, and that they should display quality journalism (not mimeo sheets, for instance). Respondents could rate each journal on a five-point scale from "nearly worthless" to "very valuable" or could indicate that they were not familiar (NF) with the journal. For ease of interpretation we have combined the two "worthless" and the two "valuable" categories and omitted the "uncertain" responses.

JOURNAL	WORTHLESS	VALUABLE	NF
Our Firm Foundation	5%	12%	79%
The Layworker	8%	6%	81%
Spectrum	6%	9%	78%
Good News Unlimited	3%	6%	86%

Unfortunately for the research–as the chart makes clear–the vast majority of Adventists were not familiar with any of these journals. This means that too few people are included for meaningful analysis. However, those who perceive the journals as valuable may be strong in their convictions and have influence in the church, particularly in the case of *Our Firm Foundation* where 12 percent in support may be worth noting by church leaders.

A Theory of Religious Commitment

We have presented the multidimensional measures of religion as separate scales or items. It will be helpful to find a way to integrate them into a whole. The model of religious commitment proposed in this study uses the theory of norm conformity as a basis for understanding the pattern of relationship among the religious variables.[16]

The basic assumption of this model is that religious ideas and behaviors are to be interpreted as normative consequences of religious group involvement. The same principles that govern the organization and life of other organizations are applicable to religious groups. As members of a specific community, believers develop a common identity, share common ideas, and conform their actions to the expectations of the group. These expectations, which develop into social norms and values, are sustained by various sanctions and reinforcements. Within a religious sectarian group, such as Seventh-day Adventism, group norms create a distinct culture which distinguishes it from other communities within the larger society.[17]

The theory begins by suggesting that religious commitment is an expression of public ritual participation, for it is in the process of such participation that religious values are made normative for the group. This is especially true of church attendance, for it is in the context of worship that the essence of the group becomes an imposing objective reality to the participants.

Socialization to the identity and norms of the group is also established through participation in certain rituals which call for commitment from individuals, such as financial support of the church and time volunteered to its programs. Leaders are chosen on the basis of their proven records of having assimilated well the norms and expectations of the religious community. Furthermore, a major function of leaders is to nurture and reinforce conformity to the traditions and values of the group.

What leads people to join and become active participants in a religious community such as Adventism? Research on recruitment to new religious movements has supported the theory of group attachment by establishing the essential role that interpersonal bonds play in attracting new converts. When such bonds exist between members of the group and the potential convert, greater likelihood exists that the new recruit will become involved. Potential members are also more likely to be drawn to the ideology of a group because of their ties with current representatives. Further research suggests that these principles are operative in older religions also.[18]

Adventism as a sectarian community has had a heightened emphasis on the evangelization of nonbelievers. For the most part, Adventists have used an ideological approach–the logic of Biblical truth. The research suggests that while ideology does play a role in the winning of converts, it is secondary to the interpersonal bonding process. Religious knowledge particular to Adventist theology occurs mainly after socialization into the group takes place. Religious beliefs take on significance only as they are tied to networks of social relationships.

One of the first tasks when one becomes part of a religious community is to learn about the new family–its belief system, history, behaviors expected of members, and the nature of the religious experience that one is expected to have. Consequently, orthodox beliefs are internalized and accepted as a result of intense socialization.

Religious experience also comes as a direct effect of involvement and as an indirect effect through orthodoxy. Durkheim's notion of "collective effervescence" helps us to understand how public participation can lead to an experiential encounter. He argued that religious experiences resulted from communal influence. It is in the group that we learn the "appropriate" way to experience the Divine and what manifestations of the sacred to expect.[19]

Chapter 6

In a religious gathering, emotions are heightened as a result of congregational singing, participation in ritual, liturgy, or a persuasive sermon. One observes the behavior of other participants and the reinforcement which such behavior brings. One hears of the history and present experience which characterize the life of the community. These linkages help to explain both public and private religious experiences. Not only is one more likely to experience God within the context of public worship but also indirectly through the private context of one's meditation on religious truth.

The devotional dimension represents the normative consequence of public involvement. Involvement nurtures orthodox beliefs, which lead to a subjective experience, which in turn leads to an interest in maintaining this experience through private devotional activities. Involvement then affects devotional commitment directly and indirectly. Devotional activities are not just normative prescribed behaviors which define group membership, but they also sustain religious experience and beliefs. Practices such as Bible reading and prayer function to make sense of religious experience. The use of a particular language and symbolism which are specific to the community contributes to the reinforcement of the identity of the community.

The religious expressions of commitment we have discussed also contribute to the development of a religious orientation. An intrinsic orientation integrates the various dimensions of religion into the daily experiences of life in such a way as to bestow meaning and purpose to existence. An extrinsic orientation is likely to represent a fragmented and compartmentalized religious commitment.

Religious involvement shapes the orientation both directly and indirectly through orthodoxy, experience, and devotion. Intrinsic orientation is facilitated when believers integrate their religious commitment into their daily lives in order to make life happier and more meaningful by providing ultimate answers to existential questions. People who are more involved with their religion are more likely to hold strong convictions, have subjective experiences, and participate in devotional activities, all of which contribute to the creation and maintenance of a sacred world view.

A mature religious orientation is also dependent on religious involvement. Since this orientation represents an open-minded outlook, it is expected that orthodoxy may have a negative effect on maturity. On the other hand, it is expected that religious experience and devotional practices will have positive direct effects on maturity as well as indirect effects through religious involvement. The maturity scale seeks to combine the integrative function of intrinsic religiosity with an emphasis on open-mindedness and a search for truth.

Religion is fundamentally a meaning system which seeks to make sense of the complexities of life. Life's experiences which touch the person deeply trigger the capacity for hopefulness and are recorded in that aspect of the personality called the imagination. We experience the holy through the imagination. Religious participation, beliefs, experience, devotional activities, and orientations produce images and narratives which give shape to the religious imagination.[20]

In accordance with group conformity theory then, religious imagination is shaped and developed within the context of community. The process of sharing and hearing Biblical narratives, faith pilgrimages, and worship experiences combines with one's personal stories to provide a distinct awareness of the Holy and one's unique images of the Divine. The person's images of God, then, are a consequence of prior religious experiences and commitments and are related to the degree of communal attachment.

Thus religious involvement, beliefs, subjective experience, devotional behaviors, orientations, motivations, and imagination are all related and in their totality define what it means to be religious. But the way the various elements are blended into the whole is unique for each individual. No two people are religious in exactly the same way. This variation is what makes it possible for us to study the effects of various styles of religiosity on other aspects of the life–in this study political and social attitudes. Before we turn to that, however, we need to consider the effect of background characteristics on ways of being religious.

References

[1] For those readers who are interested in details such as research design, drawing the sample, questionnaire construction, data collection, and response rates, this information is included in the appendix.

[2] Charles Y. Glock, "On the Study of Religious Commitment," *Religious Education Research Supplement* 57 (July-August 1962): 98-110.

³For example, see Morton King and Richard Hunt, "Measuring the Religious Variable: National Replication," *Journal for the Scientific Study of Religion* 14 (March 1975): 13-22 for the culminating article of nearly a decade of study and publication.

⁴All percentages are rounded to the nearest whole number, and missing values (those who did not answer that particular question) are eliminated before calculations, making 100% stand for those who actually answered the question.

⁵It is certainly possible that those who were active in their congregations were more likely to return the questionnaire than those who were not, suggesting that the rate of involvement for all American members may not be as high. See appendix for response rates.

⁶J. Milton Yinger, "A Structural Examination of Religion," *Journal for the Scientific Study of Religion* 8 (Spring 1969): 88-99.

⁷Peter L. Benson and Dorothy Williams, *Religion on Capital Hill: Myths and Realities* (New York: Harper & Row, 1982).

⁸David C. Leege and Michael R. Welch, "The Roots of Political Alignment: Examining the Relationship between Religion and Politics among Catholic Parishioners," paper presented to the American Political Science Association, Washington, DC, August 1986.

⁹Michael R. Welch and David C. Leege, "Religious Predictors of Catholic Parishioners' Sociopolitical Attitudes: Devotional Style, Closeness to God, Imagery, and

Agentic/Communal Religious Identity," *Journal for the Scientific Study of Religion* 27 (December 1988): 536-552. Quotation from p. 542.

[10] Gordon W. Allport, *Personality and Social Encounter* (Boston: Beacon Press, 1960); "Religious Context of Prejudice," *Journal for the Scientific Study of Religion* 5 (Fall 1966): 447-457.

[11] Dean R. Hoge, "A Validated Intrinsic Religious Motivation Scale," *Journal for the Scientific Study of Religion* 11 (December 1972): 369-376.

[12] Gordon W. Allport, *The Individual and His Religion* (New York: Macmillan, 1950), 57.

[13] Ibid., 72.

[14] Roger L. Dudley and Robert J. Cruise, "Measuring Religious Maturity: A Proposed Scale," *Review of Religious Research* 32 (December 1990): 97-109.

[15] Andrew M. Greeley, "Religious Imagery as a Predictor Variable in the General Social Survey," paper presented to the Society for the Scientific Study of Religion, Chicago, October 1984; idem, *Religious Change in America* (Cambridge, MA: Harvard University Press, 1989).

[16] John M. Finney, "A Theory of Religious Commitment," *Sociological Analysis* 39 (Spring 1978): 19-35.

[17] Richard H. White, "Toward a Theory of Religious Influence," *Pacific Sociological Review* 11 (1968): 23-28.

[18] John Lofland and Rodney Stark, "Becoming a World-

Saver: A Theory of Conversion to a Deviant Perspective," *American Sociological Review* 30 (1965): 862-875; James T. Richardson and Mary Stewart, "Conversion Process Models and the Jesus Movement," *American Behavioral Scientist* 20 (1977): 819-838. For more recent findings see Rodney Stark and William Bainbridge, *The Future of Religion* (Berkeley: University of California Press, 1985).

[19]Emile Durkheim, *The Elementary Forms of Religious Life* (Glencoe, IL: The Free Press, 1957).

[20]See Andrew M. Greeley, *The Religious Imagination* (New York: Sadlier, 1981).

Chapter 7

Social Sources of Religious Commitment

hy does such a great variety of religious expressions exist and flourish? Why have so many different denominations and sects arisen? Proponents of the various groups tend to defend their uniqueness on theological grounds. Social scientists have pointed to other explanations.

More than a half century ago, Niebuhr, in what has become a classic analysis, set forth the theory of sectarian origins and movement toward denominationalism and proposed the primacy of social rather than religious factors as the basis of the nation's religious pluralism. Niebuhr suggested that nonreligious factors such as social class, race, national origins, and regionalism were the decisive forces behind the structure of American religion. For example, it is easily observable that upper-class people are over-represented among certain mainline Protestant denominations like the Episcopalians and Presbyterians and that the lower working class is found disproportionately among the Pentecostal religions.[1]

Our interest in the social sources of religious commitment is to determine to what degree differences in religious commitment among Seventh-day Adventists can be attributed to background or demographic variables. This analysis, unlike that of Niebuhr's, is not a comparative one between denominations, but a within-group analysis of a single denomination. Are the various religious dimensions of Adventists (as discussed in chapter 6) related to certain social characteristics? If so, to what extent is the religious influence on political and social attitudes an indirect influence from social sources? In this chapter we attempt to answer the first question. The second is dealt with later (chapter 10). Several theories are briefly explored before examining data from this study.

Deprivation of Social Status

Social theorists frequently have interpreted religious involvement as a response to an individual's failure to find satisfaction and reward from his/her participation in the larger society.[2] They have argued that social systems create needs which lead to religious activity and that, for the poor, this activity provides a release from suffering. Religious commitment, then, offers the poor and marginal an alternative world view where they can find a sense of community and self-affirmation, escaping an alienated, secular society that judges them unfavorably.

This relationship was demonstrated vividly a half-century ago in a classic and oft-cited study in the sociology of religion by Liston Pope.[3] Pope contrasted the emotion-packed religion in the churches of the underpaid and bleak-lived laborers in the cotton mills of a North Carolina town with the prosaic religion of the middle-class uptown folks. He noted that the millhands, at the lower end of the socioeconomic scale, "substitute religious status for social status." Members of mill churches were likely to say something like: "I may not be high society, but I'm on God's first string," or "I may not have a big house, a fancy car, and a college education, but I've got what's really important–I've got true religion." Pope observed that: "Excluded from secular society, they set up a religious society of their own, in which standards of membership are more rigid than those of the general culture that has ignored them."[4]

Studies of religious commitment in the general population and among church members have yielded mixed support for the deprivation hypothesis. A common finding is that socioeconomic status is positively related to church attendance. In contrast with religious activity, religious experience has been associated more frequently with low social status. Orthodox religious beliefs are also most prevalent among the lower status groups.[5]

Consequently, socioeconomic status may be a better predictor of the *type* rather than the *level* of religious commitment. Demerath has produced data that show that the higher social classes are more likely to express their religion in cultic (church attendance and organizational participation) and cognitive (religious knowledge) ways, whereas the lower social classes tend to express religion devotionally and experientially.[6]

One of the reasons why the research may have produced mixed results is the difficulty of measuring the construct of deprivation. Deprivation may be more a matter of perception and comparison with others than an objective socioeconomic standard. Along this line, Glock has identified five types of deprivation: (1) *economic deprivation* consists of limited income and access to the material necessities of life; (2) *social deprivation* refers to the relative absence of such societal rewards as prestige, power, and status; (3) *organismic deprivation* refers to lessened physical and mental health and abilities; (4) *ethical deprivation* exists when persons come to feel that the dominant values and norms of society no longer provide them with a meaningful way of organizing their lives (anomie); (5) *psychic deprivation* results from a lack of psychic rewards–the person does not feel satisfied or really accepted.[7]

More recent research has shown that low levels of education and economic status are strongly related to sectarian religious attachment.[8] One can argue that persons with higher socioeconomic status are people who tend to be more exposed to the influence of "functional rationalization" by virtue of their vocations. Those in higher economic classes tend to be more heavily represented in management careers and the professions which demand knowledge of bureaucratic rational procedures and values. Also, higher education is more likely to expose people to a multiplicity of world views and values (pluralism), which increases one's acceptance and toleration of diverse cultural views and life styles. Thus higher education tends to reduce one's level of commitment to a monopolistic faith such as that held by Seventh-day Adventists.

On the other hand, higher education and social status may not always have a secularizing effect on religious commitment. For example, educated people tend to be selected more often to positions of leadership within religious communities, thus contributing to the salience and internalization of religious values. Such responsibility may also promote more faithful attendance. Having attended an Adventist institution of higher learning may well have a positive effect on the maintenance of religious values. Finally, particular motivations of higher-status individuals may lead them to see their vocations as opportunities to influence society for good or to share their particular faith.

The deprivation theory then would lead us to expect that those Adventists who have experienced socioeconomic deprivation will be more strongly com-mitted to their religion, especially in the ideological, experiential, and devotional dimensions. Conversely, those from higher economic and educational levels will be less committed except in the area of organizational activity. We would expect that the social status variables will predict different measures of religious commitment differently. For example, the effect of higher social status, including education, may lead individuals to de-mythologize the unique beliefs of Adventism and yet express high levels of religious involvement.

Deprivation as Minority

Deprivation as used in this study moves beyond strict measures of social class to include innate characteristics, such as gender or race, which may be useful in explaining religious commitment. The religious expressions of women and racial minorities may result from their exclusion from particular social institutions and occupational and leadership roles. Thus for women and ethnic minorities involvement in religious institutions and ideologies may provide compensation for their social poverty and relative powerlessness.

In addition, for racial minorities, religious institutions offer an opportunity to "legitimately" participate in social organizations, and since many churches continue to be largely segregated, they offer opportunities to assume leadership roles unavailable in integrated secular institutions. Moreover, ethnic churches represent ethnic enclaves wherein primary relationships are maintained and wherein otherworldly compensators provide solace to conditions of deprivation and anomie.[9]

The greater religiosity of women has been frequently observed. National opinion surveys have consistently shown women to be more likely than men to attend church frequently, to express orthodox religious beliefs, to consider their religious beliefs "very important," and to report having religious experiences.[10] This greater commitment has been assumed to have resulted from status deprivation flowing from gender inequalities in society. The disparity between the two genders does not seem to be shrinking despite the recent gains of women in society.

Factors other than deprivation may explain some of the "gender gap." Traditionally, women have been more concerned with the family and child-rearing, both of which are topics frequently discussed and emphasized within the church. Women have also been the backbone of voluntary organizations, including the church, presumably because they were not as likely to be engaged full time in the work force. The great increase in women working outside the home may tend to reduce the greater religious commitment of females.

It is also a common finding that racial minorities tend to be more religious than Whites. The church has played a major role in the Black community since the nineteenth century. Far more than White churches, Black congregations have been responsible for the social, economic, and political life of their members.[11] Recent national opinion polls show that more non-Whites than Whites consider their religious beliefs "very important," accept fundamentalist religious beliefs, and are active church members.[12]

Blacks are not the only minority demonstrating greater religious commitment. Within American Catholicism, Hispanics have been found to have greater levels of institutional attachment, more frequent devotional activities, and firmer adherence to conservative religious values than non-Hispanics.[13] This trend has also been demonstrated among Hispanics and Blacks in the Adventist church.[14]

The lower socioeconomic status and educational levels of minorities and the social deprivations they have experienced presumably have motivated them to seek refuge from a hostile world. Consequently, minorities are more likely to seek otherworldly compensators through involvement in religion, especially forms which appeal to the deep emotional life. Moreover, ethnic churches provide the context where primary social relationships can be maintained, creating a sense of community and continuity, establishing a hedge against the individualizing forces of modernity.

Given these dynamics, we might expect that female Adventists are more likely to be religiously committed than male Adventists. We might further expect that ethnic minority Adventists (especially Blacks and Hispanics) are more likely to be religiously committed than White Adventists.

Life Cycle and Religious Commitment

Another category of explanations stems from the observed relationship between aging and religious commitment. One of the difficulties in interpreting differences in religious commitment observed among age groups in cross-sectional surveys is that differences between age cohorts can be explained by either life-cycle changes or varying generational experiences. Life-cycle explanations emphasize that people of the same age share the same physical and mental capabilities, social status, and opportunities. These similarities give rise to similar needs and expressions. Generational theories, on the other hand, emphasize that people of the same age have been influenced by social events or the historic period in which they reached maturity.[15] Both of these theories no doubt play a part.

For example, a life-cycle explanations for adolescent rejection of religion is found in emancipation theory.[16] Growing out of developmental psychology, this view holds that a prime task of adolescence is to gain emotional independence and at least the promise of financial independence from parents and other authority figures. In this process of emancipation the young person makes a symbolic, if subconscious, statement of independence by effecting a psychological separation from the parents. This may be most effectively accomplished by rejecting the religious values of parents in homes where religion is prominent.[17] On the other hand, increasing secularization, the general decay of traditional values, and the sexual revolution might be posited as generational explanations for the phenomenon.

For parents with young children, religious commitment has been thought to rise as a result of an interest in securing moral training for the children. Those individuals who have rejected or neglected religion as youth find a new appeal in it once they marry and have children. It is argued that their concern for the welfare and character of their offspring may lead them to seek religious education and participate more readily in religious activities.[18]

Life-cycle interpretations suggest several reasons for an increase in religious commitment among the elderly. Religious feelings, beliefs, and activity increase over the life cycle due to the need to compensate for the growing frustrations and losses associated with aging and the increasing imminence of death. Christian ideologies offer comfort with their promises of immortality.[19] Also, religious organizations provide the elderly with an opportunity to make new associations and to find substitutes for lost friends and family members.

General population surveys generally do demonstrate an increase in religious commitment with age. A 1977-78 Gallup study showed a continual increase in church attendance between the ages of 18 and 50. For example, 32 percent of respondents between the ages of 18 and 24 reported that they had attended church in the previous week compared with 42 percent of those between the ages of 30 and 39 and 48 percent of those 50 years or older. The report also showed an increase over the life cycle in the percentage of respondents reporting that they were active members in a church or synagogue. Active membership ranged from a low of 36 percent for those between the ages of 18 and 24 to a high of 61 percent for those 50 years or older. The percentages indicating that their religious beliefs were "very important" and expressing "a great deal" of confidence in organized religion increased continuously over the life cycle as well.

All of this would lead us to expect that the older members in our sample would display greater religious commitment in each of the various dimensions that were measured. In light of the expectations stated so far in this chapter, what do the empirical data reveal?

Demographic Determinants

To determine the influence of background variables on religious commitment, we took each of the measures of religion that we employed–orthodoxy, religious experience, church-related behaviors, devotional behaviors, salience, foundational world view, intrinsic-extrinsic motivation, religious maturity, and religious imagery–and compared them with various demographic groups. The grouping variables were gender, religious background, marital status, age, ethnicity, family income, and level of formal education. For example, we asked whether or not significant differences in orthodoxy existed between males and females or whether different levels of devotional behavior could be found among Asians, Blacks, Hispanics, and Whites.

The statistical tool for this analysis was Analysis of Variance (ANOVA), an appropriate procedure where the independent variable (e.g., ethnicity) can be conceptualized as two or more discrete groups and where the dependent variable (e.g., orthodoxy) is a continuous measurement. The F-ratio yields the probability that the differences between the group means could have occurred by chance if no actual difference between these means was present in the population from which the sample was drawn. Probabilities less than .05 (five chances out of one hundred) are deemed *significant*, and differences between group means are declared real. If the independent variable has only two levels (e.g., gender), it is obvious that the difference is between these two (male and female). If the independent variable has more than two levels (e.g., age) multiple range tests indicate just which groups are truly different. For the variable "ethnicity" we employed two different groupings. First, we used the five separate groups listed on the survey. Then, because the numbers in the minority groups were small, we combined them to make just two groups–Whites and minorities. The results were the same for every religious variable except devotional behaviors and intrinsic motivation. Certain limitations in the data make it necessary to offer the following conclusions with caution. For a discussion of these limitations, see the appendix.

Orthodoxy. Significant differences for orthodoxy or beliefs were found for marital status, age group, family income, and level of formal education.

On marital status, the widowed were significantly more committed to Adventist beliefs than either the never married or the presently married. Perhaps the sorrow these members have experienced has drawn them closer to the church and encouraged them to cling more closely to their beliefs in a search for hope. More likely, this variable is being confounded by age. The widowed are likely to be older, and age is positively associated with orthodoxy.

On age, both those 51 to 65 years and those over 65 years were more orthodox than those 20 to 35 years and those 36 to 50 years. So few of the respondents were under 20 years that valid comparisons with this group are difficult. These findings support the expectations which were set forth.

On family income, as the income level rose, the mean for orthodoxy went down in a consistent and linear pattern. Those with family incomes of $50,000 or over were significantly lower on orthodoxy than all other groups, and those with incomes between $25,000 and $50,000 were lower than those with incomes under $10,000. Again, this supports the theory of deprivation.

Our other measure of socioeconomic status is level of formal education. Those with graduate professional training were less orthodox than groups with less education. Those whose education had terminated before high-school graduation were more strongly committed to Adventist beliefs than those with some college, a four-year college degree, or graduate professional training. Again, these findings are in the expected direction. No differences in orthodoxy were found for gender, religious background, or ethnicity (even when the four minorities were grouped together).

Religious experience. Significant differences on religious experience were found for five grouping variables–tied for the most of any. They were religious background, marital status, age group, ethnic background, and family income. No differences were discovered for gender or level of education.

On religious background, those not brought up in an Adventist home were more likely to affirm an experiential religion than those who were. Presumably, being a first-generation Adventist is more likely to lead to personal emotional involvement. Those who have grown up in the church and have not had to make the same kind of personal choice may be more casual about their religion.

On marital status, those who had never married were lower on experiential religion than the other groups (presently married, widowed, and divorced). Perhaps the joys and sorrows of these experiences have increased the emotional capacity of the latter. However, religious experience is correlated with age, and the never married are younger on the whole than the other groups.

On age, both those 51 to 65 years and those over 65 years were more experiential in their religion than those 20 to 35 years and those 36 to 50 years. Again, these findings support the expectations which were set forth.

On ethnicity, Blacks were higher on religious experience than Whites. This is another expected finding given the deprivation theory and the Black experience in America. Minorities as a group were more likely to score higher on the Experiential Scale than Whites.

On family income, those with incomes of $50,000 or over were significantly lower than all other groups on experiential religion. This finding continues to support the deprivation theory.

Church-related behaviors. Significant differences for church-related behaviors (ritual dimension or involvement) were found for gender, age group, and ethnic background.

On gender, males were more likely to be involved than females. This may reflect the tendency to place males in leadership roles and the increased financial support that comes from the greater earning power of males.

On age group, all groups above 36 years were more involved than those in the 20 to 35 years group, and those over 65 years were more involved than those in the 36 to 50 years groups. Ritual commitment has been shown to heighten with age.

On ethnic background, both Asians and Blacks (as well as minorities as a group) were more involved than Whites. This provides another support for the theoretical background.

The differences on family income did not reach the .05 level of significance, but they were very close at .061. Here, those who had incomes of $16,000 to $25,000 were more involved than those with lower incomes and those who had over $50,000. The very poor tend not to be involved in cultic ways while the wealthy tend toward less commitment. It is the middle group that carries the church.

Devotional practices. Significant differences for devotional practices were found for three grouping variables–marital status, age group, and ethnicity.

On marital status, the widowed and those presently married were more regular in devotions than the never married. While painful losses and family responsibilities may create a sense of need that leads one to prayer and Bible study, it is also likely that this finding is confounded by the age variable.

On age, those in the group of 20 to 35 years were less likely to engage in devotional behavior than those in any of the older groups, and those over 65 years were also more likely to be regular in devotions than those between 36 and 50 years. Thus, the theory of life-cycle religion is again supported.

On ethnicity, no significant differences were found when the minorities were grouped separately. When put together, however, minorities as a group were more frequent in their devotions than were Whites.

Salience. Significant differences for salience, or importance of religious faith, were found for three grouping variables–religious background, marital status, and age group.

On religious background, those not raised in an Adventist home were more likely to affirm the importance of their faith. Again, we see the contrast between personal choice and inherited faith.

On marital status, those who had never married considered their faith less important than did members of the other three groups (married, widowed, and divorced). As noted before, we cannot rule out the correlation with age.

On age, those 20 to 35 years did not place as much importance on their faith as did those who were in all the older groups. Those over 65 also considered faith more important than did those in the 36 to 50 age group.

Foundational world view. Significant differences for foundational world view were found only for gender. Males were more likely to be communitarian, or at least mixed, and females were more likely to be individualistic. It should be remembered, however, that most of the subjects, whatever the gender, were scored individualistic.

Intrinsic-extrinsic motivation. Significant differen-ces for intrinsic-extrinsic motivation were found for five grouping variables–tying with religious experience for the most. They were religious background, marital status, age group, ethnic background, and family income. From the discussion earlier in this chapter, it is evident that no adequate theoretical framework has been developed for how intrinsic-extrinsic motivation might be expected to relate to demographic variables. However, since intrinsic religion has been shown to correlate with orthodoxy, and we might expect it to relate to devotional practices and to those church-related behaviors that go beyond mere attendance (e.g., financial support), we could predict similar patterns to that of the other measures of religious commitment. Indeed, Kirkpatrick and Hood have recently suggested that the intrinsic scale is basically a measure of religious commitment rather than an assessment of motivation or a personality construct.[20]

On religious background, those who were not raised in Adventist homes tended to be higher on the intrinsic scale.

On marital status, those never married averaged lower on intrinsic than the other groups, and the widowed were higher than the presently married.

On age group, those 20 to 35 years averaged lower on intrinsic than all three older groups, and those 36 to 50 years were lower than the two older groups.

On ethnic background, Blacks were higher on the intrinsic scale than either Asians or Whites. However, when minorities were treated as a group, no significant difference was found between them and the Whites.

On annual family income, those making over $50,000 were lower on the intrinsic scale than all of the lower groups.

Thus, demographic differences on the intrinsic-extrinsic scale did follow the same patterns seen for other measures of religious commitment.

Religious maturity. Significant differences for religious maturity were found only for gender. Males averaged higher maturity scores than females. However, level of education was very close to significance at .064. Those with professional graduate education averaged higher maturity scores than those who had some college or a four-year college degree.

Religious imagery. Significant differences for religious imagery were found for gender and family income. Females were more likely than males to picture God in "graceful" images. Those who had annual incomes of $50,000 or more averaged lower on the grace scale than most of the groups earning less.

Chapter 7

Conclusions

Thus, the empirical data from this study support, in general, the theoretical framework presented earlier in this chapter. Not every background variable differentially predicts every measure of religious commitment. But no finding goes against the theory and many confirm it. The evidence is especially strong for age and the life-cycle theory. Socioeconomic status, including income and education, is quite well supported also. Some support is found for ethnicity although the evidence here is much weaker.

It was hypothesized that ethnic minorities would show higher levels of religious commitment than Whites. This was established for religious experience, church involvement, devotional behaviors, and intrinsic orientation but not for the other religious variables such as orthodoxy. It also was primarily related to the greater commitment of Blacks rather than ethnic minorities in general, although Whites almost always had the lowest means even if the differences were not significant.

One of the factors that may have weakened ethnicity as a cause of commitment is the fact that the minorities in this sample were not significantly different from the Whites with respect to income and level of education, thus reducing the deprivation explanation. An alternative hypothesis which may offer an explanation for the relationships that were found is that ethnic communities function to solidify ethnic ties and to create community among members, irrespective of their social status.

Under this formulation, since most ethnic groups in the Adventist church worship in segregated congregations, religious experience becomes an expression of communal identity and commitment.[21] Ethnic religious communities function as "communities of memory," reinforcing primary group ties and providing a system of meaning and belonging.[22]

The finding that older Adventists are more likely to be committed on most of the dimensions of religion than younger members suggests a significant generation gap. Younger Adventists in this sample tend to have higher incomes and more formal education. They represent the "new class," white-collar professionals whose encounter with rational bureaucratic norms and thought patterns has significantly altered their religious expressions.[23] If this proves to be a generational rather than a life-cycle effect, the church faces serious considerations for the future. As committed older members who have been the backbone of support for the church pass off the scene, will the "new class" take up the mantle with equal commitment?

Socioeconomic status–as measured by income and level of education–has been shown to be negatively related to a number of measures of religious commitment. This higher socioeconomic status group, that has been labeled the "new class," is primarily young, male, and White. It is this group that is less likely to accept the unique teachings of the Seventh-day Adventist Church. Consistent with the theoretical perspective presented earlier, exposure to cultural pluralism and functional rationalization significantly diminishes the unique claims of sectarian religion.

Now that we have examined the religion of American Adventists and its social sources, we turn to the other great area of interest to this study–their attitudes and behaviors concerning public issues and politics.

References

[1] H. Richard Niebuhr, *The Social Sources of Denominationalism* (New York: Meridian Books, 1929). For a more recent analysis on the social sources of denominationalism see Wade Clark Roof and William McKinney, *American Mainline Religion* (New Brunswick, N.J.: Rutgers University Press, 1987), 106-47.

[2] Rodney Stark and Charles Y. Glock, *American Piety: The Nature of Religious Commitment* (Berkeley, CA: University of California Press, 1968).

[3] Liston Pope, *Millhands and Preachers* (New Haven: Yale University Press, 1942).

[4] Ibid., 137-138.

[5] Gallup Public Opinion Survey, "Religion in America," 1979.

[6] N. J. Demerath III, *Social Class in American Protestantism* (Chicago: Rand McNally, 1965).

[7] Charles Y. Glock, "The Role of Deprivation in the Origin and Evolution of Religious Groups," in *Religion and Social Conflict* ed., Robert Lee and Martin E. Marty (New York: Oxford University Press, 1964), 24-36.

[8]Rodney Stark and William S. Bainbridge, *The Future of Religion* (Berkeley, CA: University of California Press, 1985).

[9]Phillip Hammond, "Religion and the Persistence of Identity," *Journal for the Scientific Study of Religion* 27 (March 1988): 1-11; Edwin I. Hernandez and Roger L. Dudley, "Persistence of Religion through Primary Group Ties among Hispanic Seventh-day Adventist Young People," *Review of Religious Research* 32 (December 1990)157-172.

[10]Michael Argyle, *Religious Behavior* (Glencoe, IL: The Free Press, 1958); Gallup Public Opinion Survey (1979).

[11]C. Eric Lincoln and Lawrence H. Mamiya, *The Black Church in the African American Experience* (Durham, NC: Duke University Press, 1990).

[12]Gallup Public Opinion Survey (1979).

[13]Office of Pastoral Research, *Hispanics in New York: Religious, Cultural, and Social Experiences* (New York: Archdiocese of New York, 1982).

[14]Roger L. Dudley and Des Cummings, Jr., *Adventures in Church Growth* (Hagerstown, MD: Review and Herald Publishing Association, 1983), 51-57.

[15]Robert Wuthnow, "Recent Patterns of Secularization: A Problem of Generations?" *American Sociological Review* 41 (1976): 850-867.

[16]Roger L. Dudley and Margaret G. Dudley, "Transmission of Religious Values from Parents to Adolescents," *Review of Religious Research* 28 (September 1986): 3-15.

¹⁷Roger L. Dudley, "'Adolescent Heresy': The Rejection of Parental Religious Values," *Andrews University Seminary Studies* 21 (Spring 1983): 51-59.

¹⁸Widick Schroeder, "Age Cohorts, the Family Cycle, and Participation in the Voluntary Church in America: Implications for Membership Patterns, 1950-2000," *Chicago Theological Seminary Register* 65 (1975): 13-28.

¹⁹David Moberg, "Religiosity in Old Age," *The Gerontologist* 5 (1965): 78-87.

²⁰Lee A. Kirkpatrick and Ralph W. Hood, Jr., "Intrinsic-Extrinsic Religious Orientation: The Boon or Bane of Contemporary Psychology of Religion?" *Journal for the Scientific Study of Religion* 29 (December 1990): 442-462.

²¹Robert Wuthnow, *Meaning and Moral Order: Exploration in Cultural Analysis* (Berkeley, CA: University of California Press, 1987).

²²Robert Bellah, Richard Madsen, William Sullivan, Ann Swidler, and Steven Tipton, *Habits of the Heart* (Berkeley, CA: University of California Press, 1985). Hernandez and Dudley, 157-72.

²³Barbara Hargrove, *The Emerging New Class: Implications for Church and Society* (New York: Pilgrim Press, 1986).

Chapter 8

The Politics of American Adventists

Some years ago the senior author was invited to join the working force in a particular conference. As the conference president chatted with him about the new position, he remarked: "You'll like it here. This state is a good place for Adventists to live."

"I'm sure I will," the author replied, "but why is this state good for Adventists?"

"For one thing," explained the president, "it's politically conservative."

With the passage of years, other factors are no longer remembered, but the author has often mused about this one. Are Adventists more conservative than the general public in politics, economics, or social issues? Are they highly likely to vote Republican (or not to vote at all)? Do they espouse capitalism as a desired form of government? Are they "doves" or "hawks"? Do they have a tendency to oppose governmental aid to the needy and downtrodden?

To probe the areas represented by these questions, our survey included items on attitudes toward public issues, preference for political party, political orientation, and recent voting behavior. This chapter analyzes the responses in an attempt to answer the question: What are American Adventists like politically?

Attitudes toward Public Issues

To measure positions held on various current issues (in 1988) we selected eighteen statements and asked our subjects to respond to each on a five-point scale from "strongly oppose" to "strongly favor." A list of more than twice this length was originally prepared, and, because of space limitations, was reduced to the present size by attempting to select a battery of items that would be representative (rather than exhaustive) of the most-debated public concerns of the day.

One major issue that is missing is abortion. After much consideration it was decided not to include this topic because the study focuses on *public* issues. While abortion certainly has a public face, it is also greatly involved in private morality. It was feared that private morality might become confused with the public issue. For example, some might be morally opposed to abortion but oppose laws prohibiting it on the grounds that government should not interfere in moral and religious issues. Also some might favor laws to restrict abortion generally but permit it under certain circumstances (such as incest or rape). It would have taken several questions to clarify these issues, and space did not permit.

The responses to the various items may be read from the chart below. For ease of interpretation, we have combined "strongly oppose" and "somewhat oppose" into an "oppose" category and "strongly favor" and "somewhat favor" into a "favor" category. The extent to which the percentages fail to total 100 percent represents the "uncertain" response.

STATEMENT	OPPOSE	FAVOR
United States-Soviet "freeze" on the development of nuclear weapons	10%	72%
Establishment of normal, peaceful relations with Russia	6 %	79%
Increased government aid to improve the social and economic position of Blacks and other minorities	24%	52%
Elimination of all racial restrictions in housing, education, and employment	7%	81%

Chapter 8

STATEMENT	OPPOSE	FAVOR
The Equal Rights Amendment (ERA) to the Constitution which guarantees equality to women	22%	62%
Christians as individuals becoming involved in political action (run for office, work for a candidate, etc.)	35%	41%
Churches as corporate entities becoming involved in political action (e.g., issuing position statements)	70%	14%
A constitutional amendment to permit prayer and/or Bible reading in public schools	47%	38%
Increased spending for national defense	49%	21%
Military aid to the Nicaraguan "Contras"	44%	23%
Government-sponsored insurance for elderly in nursing homes	7%	75%
Construction of Strategic Defense Initiative (Star Wars) to ward off possible nuclear attack	35%	34%

STATEMENT	OPPOSE	FAVOR
Appointment of conservative, strict-constructionist justices (such as Rehnquist, Scalia, and Bork) to the US Supreme Court	35%	22%
Control of crime by tougher laws and "stiffer" sentences	8%	81%
Withdrawal of the United States from the United Nations	55%	14%
Registration of all firearms	21%	63%
Regarding capitalism or free enterprise as that form of government most in harmony with Biblical Christianity	11%	53%
Capital punishment (the death penalty) for certain classes of dangerous criminals	18%	62%

Conservative-Liberal Trends

In order to perceive some sort of pattern to these findings, let us organize them into a conservative-liberal framework. Nine of the statements are worded as typically "liberal" statements; the other nine as typically "conservative." Below are shown the liberal statements arranged in the order of support suggested above (total responses of "somewhat favor" and "strongly favor"). Statements are abbreviated to their kernel idea.

Favoring "liberal" positions

Eliminate racial restrictions in housing, etc.	81%
Establish peaceful relations with Russia	79%
Government insurance for elderly in nursing homes	75%
U.S.-Soviet freeze on nuclear weapons	72%
Registration of all firearms	63%
Equality for women (ERA)	62%
Government aid to improve position of minorities	52%
Individual Christians becoming involved in politics	41%
Churches becoming involved in political action	14%

On seven of these nine issues the majority favored the statement–an indication of inclination toward liberalism on the politico-social front. Note that American Adventists are most likely to favor the liberal stance on socio-economic and peace issues and most likely to forsake it on strictly political concerns. The least support was given to churches becoming involved, with 70 percent opposing this item. It is as if the members were saying: "We may agree that some of these positions are good and worthwhile if they are put into operation by 'secular' people, but we are not sure that Adventists should help to make them a reality, and we are quite certain that the church should not take sides." This seems to reflect the historic Adventist stance on separation of church and state. It also echoes the theme that the work of the church is primarily to save sinners and prepare them for the world to come, not to improve their lot in this world. Incidentally, the involvement of churches in the political process has historically been considered a liberal stance, as we have demonstrated earlier, but with the rise of the New Religious Right, conservatives have entered this arena *en masse*. Thus the rejection of this statement by the majority of Adventists should be seen not as political conservatism but as theological separatism.

The fact that government aid to improve the position of minorities gathered only a very narrow majority while at the same time strong support was given to eliminating racial restrictions and providing government insurance for nursing-home care suggests that it is not latent racism that held down the percentage favoring aid to minorities. More likely, this development reflects the Adventist (and generally conservative Protestant) self-help theology with its emphasis on individual salvation. "Each person relates to God individually, and God helps those who help themselves."

The statement on the Equal Rights Amendment to the United States Constitution (ERA) is especially pertinent in view of the current struggle in the Adventist church over the role of women. Questions raised in the struggle include whether women may be properly ordained to the Gospel ministry or not and whether or not they may serve as pastors or elders of local congregations. While the questionnaire statement did not address these issues directly, earlier research has shown that pastors in North America who support the equality of women in the public arena are more likely to affirm their full equality in the ministry of the church.[1] If the same is true of lay members, the response to this statement may provide some clue as to the strength of support for women in pastoral ministry.

In light of the current relevance of this issue to the church, it may be worthwhile to give a complete breakdown on the support for the statement:

Strongly oppose	13%
Somewhat oppose	9%
Uncertain	16%
Somewhat favor	22%
Strongly favor	40%

It seems obvious that those who take either position are more likely to feel strongly than mildly about it. Thus the polarization in society–and in the church if this statement provides a clue to attitudes concerning women in ministry. The measure of support, then, suggests that women will become more acceptable as ordained pastors (at least in the United States) in the future.

This seems especially likely in view of the age grouping of our sample. Nearly half (48%) were over 50 years of age, and a quarter were over 65. Only 28 percent were 35 years or younger. Yet a constant finding in all research is that younger people are more likely to favor the rights of women and minorities than are older ones. If this "more mature" sample is as supportive of ERA as the results indicate, one could predict even higher support as the younger generation moves into leadership roles in the church. However, as is noted in chapter 10, positions on this issue are not significantly different among different demographic groupings in this sample.

If the remaining nine issues are arranged in a similar manner, the following picture emerges:

Favoring "conservative" positions

Tougher laws and stiffer sentences on crime	81%
Capital punishment for dangerous criminals	62%
Capitalism in harmony with Bible Christianity	53%
Prayer/Bible reading in public schools	38%
Strategic Defense Initiative (Star Wars)	34%
Military aid to Nicaraguan "Contras"	23%
Conservative justices on US Supreme Court	22%
Increased spending for national defense	21%
Withdrawal from United Nations	14%

In contrast to the "liberal issues," the majority of Adventists favored only three out of the nine "conservative" issues. The support was much less here, although it must not be inferred that the subjects necessarily *opposed* these other issues. The "uncertain" response was high on several of them, especially the last five (all over 30%). The two most highly favored issues deal with law and order–perhaps reflecting the heavy law orientation prominent among Adventists. The third-favored position deals with approval of capitalism as the economic system most in harmony with Biblical Christianity. This may again reflect the work ethic that grows out of a strong sense of righteous behavior. Majority support for these three statements may also indicate the increasing alignment of Adventism with the American social system–"an alternative to the Republic" in the framework of Bull and Lockhart.

    A conservative cause that fails to gain majority support is a constitutional amendment to permit prayer and Bible reading in public schools. This finding is easily explained by the historical opposition by the church to entanglement of the state with religion. Adventists believe in making religion the foundation of education, and they support a massive parochial school system from the kindergarten to the university levels to do just that. But they are wary of any government-endorsed religion. In their historic scenario of the lamblike Republic that turns into the persecuting dragon, government-sponsored prayer and Bible-reading in the schools may be the foot in the door that eventually leads to other religious legislation, government control of churches, and persecution for dissenters. The same reasoning may be operating in the meager support for the appointment of conservative, strict-constructionist, justices to the United States Supreme Court. Traditionally, it has been "liberal" justices rather than "conservative" ones who have championed individual liberties and the separation of church and state.

The other conservative items that gathered only minority support are all military and defense issues. In general, conservatives support a strong defense to protect America from "godless" systems like communism that would destroy its traditional moral and family values. Adventists would have reason to take a similar position except that they have historically been a "semi-peace church." Because of their high regard for the ten commandments–of which the sixth prohibits killing–and problems involving Sabbath military service, Adventists have tended to eschew service in the military. While the church does not enforce pacifism, it recommends that its young people do not enlist in the armed services and, if drafted, to serve in the unarmed medical branches. It is not surprising that given the tension between concern for values threatened by communism and historical noncombatance, majorities neither favored nor opposed the military and defense items, but that large proportions were undecided.

These eighteen items were combined into a Public Issues Scale. The conservative items were reversed in scoring so that a high score indicates a more liberal position and a low score a conservative one. The reliability was unacceptably low; due, no doubt, to the fact that many different concepts were being measured, and these varying concepts did not hang together on a conservative-liberal continuum for reasons described above. Therefore, we did not use a unitary scale in our analyses but, as described in chapter 9, considered individual public issues in relation to the various measures of religion.

Political Party Preference

In addition to attitudes toward public issues, we asked three questions requiring the respondent to consider directly his/her relationship to political matters. The first was: "With which political party do you most closely identify?" The answers were as follows:

Democrat	24%
Republican	44%
Independent	12%
No interest in politics	20%

While most Adventists did not consider themselves Republicans, those who did constituted the largest grouping of any political identification. Democrats were considerably behind, doing only a little better than half as well.

Since Republicans are generally considered the more conservative party, and since Adventists in this survey tended to favor more liberal issues, this finding presents somewhat of a puzzle. It seems likely that the Republican party in general may be viewed as the party of stability and status quo—the one most likely to preserve traditional moral and family values. Thus, Adventists may identify with it in general although they feel free to disagree with it on specific issues such as church-state concerns and military build-up.

It is also important that nearly a third did not identify with either party and that a fifth took no interest in politics. Again, this may reflect the historic trends in the church that lead members to conclude that Christians should not be involved in government at all but dedicate themselves to the spreading of the Gospel.

Political Orientation

Perhaps not all see a connection between a conservative-liberal framework and a choice of political party. So we asked the question more directly: "Which of the following terms best describes your political orientation?"

Conservative	34%
Moderate	37%
Liberal	5%
No opinions	24%

If we compare the 34 percent who rated themselves as conservatives with the 44 percent who identified with the Republican party, it becomes evident that a number of Republicans do not consider themselves to be conservative; a conclusion anticipated in the discussion of the preceding section. The largest grouping claimed to be moderates–a somewhat surprising finding given the almost sacred character of the word "conservative" among Adventists. Only 5 percent were bold enough to claim the "L" word. Here again, nearly a fourth showed unwillingness to engage in the political arena by expressing "no opinions."

Chapter 8

Recent Voting Behavior

It is one thing to ask for political opinions or political self-identification. It is another to chart a particular political behavior. Perhaps the behavior by which Americans best reveal their political leanings is voting for the president of the United States. This national rite sweeps the whole nation into its lengthy process and allows for more comprehensive discussion of national issues than does any other event.

Therefore, we asked: "For whom did you vote in the last presidential election?" The choices were "Reagan," "Mondale," and "didn't vote." It might be asked why 1984 rather than 1988 candidates were listed. This is because the questionnaire was constructed and data collection begun prior to the 1988 elections and, indeed, even before it was determined with certainty who the candidates would be. While we might have asked: "For whom do you intend to vote?" we felt that some might be unsure until closer to the election date or might change their minds. The accomplished fact seemed a more stable measure. Also, the Reagan-Mondale contest was clearly perceived in conservative-liberal terms, given the past records and associations of each candidate.

Only about 60 percent of the Adventists voted (probably not worse than the nation at large) with Reagan at 46 percent outpulling Mondale (15%) three to one. Either all the Republicans voted, or a fair share of the Democrats and independents went for Reagan. The latter certainly seems likely.

Why did Adventists who favored "liberal" causes and who identified themselves as moderates vote for Reagan, the conservative candidate, especially when he supported actions that would seem to bridge the separation of church and state (e.g., school prayer amendment, ambassador to the Vatican, etc.)? Several reasons may be suggested.

For one thing, Reagan swept the country at large, winning the electoral votes of all but two states. Adventists are certainly influenced by surrounding opinions and tend to agree with their fellow Americans. For another thing, other factors probably played a larger factor than religion in the Adventist vote. The economy had risen from its earlier slump, and many members were doing quite well financially. The incumbent always has a large advantage in such cases. Moreover, Mondale let it be known that he felt a tax increase was necessary. Adventists may well have voted their pocketbooks rather than their principles.

Also, Reagan was a master at articulating traditional moral and family values. These would be shared by most Adventists, many of whom might not consider by what means such values would or could be integrated into public life. Given two different candidates and a different social ferment, the election might not have been so one-sided, although, in view of the political-party identification, it is likely that the Republican would still have drawn a plurality of Adventist votes. And it is well to remember that a sizable minority (39%) of Adventist members did not vote at all, apparently preferring to abstain from the political process.

Now that we know what American Adventists are like religiously and politically, we are ready for our major research task. How does the first quality influence the second? Do variations in religious belief, experience, and practice relate to variations in political attitudes and behaviors?

Reference

[1]Roger L. Dudley, "Pastoral Views on Women in Ministry," *Adventist Review*, 4 June 1987, 17-19.

Chapter 9

How Religion Informs Political Positions

Our first step in attempting to establish a connection between religion and positions on public issues was to look for significant correlations between the Public Issues Scale and the scales measuring various aspects of religion. For those readers unfamiliar with the term, correlation refers to the "going-togetherness" of two variables. If one variable tends to go up as the second rises (e.g., school grades and intelligence scores), they are said to be *positively* correlated. If one tends to go down as the second goes up (e.g., body weight and vigorous exercise), they are said to be *negatively* correlated. If no pattern can be discovered in the changes of two variables (e.g., personal income and shoe size), they are said to be not correlated or to have *zero correlation.*

The number indicating the strength of the correlation is called the *coefficient of correlation.* Coefficients may range from -1.00 (perfect negative correlation) through 0.00 to +1.00 (perfect positive correlation). While perfect correlations may be found in the physical sciences, human behavior is so complex and multi-faceted that they are never encountered in the social and behavioral sciences. A correlation of + or - .30 to .50 is usually considered quite strong. For example, years of research indicate that the correlation between intelligence scores and school grades is about .50 (the plus sign is usually omitted). While intelligence has a strong positive influence on grades, other factors also play a part.

In chapter 8 we described how we created a Public Issues Scale from the eighteen attitude items and how it had low reliability; that is, the responses to the items did not hang together well. It was not surprising then, although disappointing, to discover no significant correlations between the Public Issues Scale and any of the measures of religion. Typically the correlations hovered around zero with only one reaching as much as .05. As noted in the last chapter, this finding reflects the fact that the public issues items do not represent a unified concept on a conservative-liberal continuum–at least not for this sample. Adventists are likely to think in a diversity of ways on these issues and answer in ways inconsistent with the construct of the scale (although perfectly consistent to their ways of thinking). As noted, such diversified responses reflect the denomination's history and peculiar experiences.

Such lack of interscale correlation does not mean, though, that the religion scales might not significantly predict positions on various individual public issues. As a matter of fact, they do. This chapter now takes up this matter, scale by scale. In most cases, two types of analysis are employed: Pearson correlations and $\underline{t}$-tests for the difference of independent means.

To save space in frequent repetitions of terms, the various public issues are referred to by short code names. The reader may find the full wording by consulting the previous chapter, but a list of code names with short descriptions is as follows:

Nuclear	Freeze on development of nuclear weapons
Russia	Normal, peaceful relations with Russia
GovernAid	Government aid to improve lot of minorities
Racial	Eliminate racial restrictions in all areas
Women	Equality for women (Equal Rights Amendment)
Politics	Christians becoming involved in politics
Position	Churches involved in political action
Prayer	Prayer/Bible reading in public schools
Defense	Increased spending for national defense
Contras	Military aid to Nicaraguan "Contras"
Elderly	Government insurance for nursing homes
SDI	Strategic Defense Initiative (Star Wars)
SupremeCourt	Conservative justices on US Supreme Court
Crime	Tougher laws and stiffer sentences on Crime
UN	Withdrawal of US from United Nations
Firearms	Registration of all firearms
Capitalism	Capitalism: system most in harmony with Bible
DeathPenalty	Capital punishment for dangerous criminals

Chapter 9

Belief or Orthodoxy

Correlations were calculated between the Belief Scale and each of the eighteen public issues items in an attempt to discover significant relationships. The word "significant" as used in empirical research does not necessarily mean "important." Rather, it is a term based on the statistical probability of a particular finding occurring by chance. It is a way of inferring whether a statistic calculated from a sample (in this case, our 419 respondents) is likely to represent a relationship of some kind in the population from which the sample was drawn (in this case, all American Adventists of 18 years or older).

In the case of correlational analysis, the question is: Given the size of the coefficient of correlation in this sample, how likely is it that the same two variables are zero correlated in the population? Or more precisely: What is the probability of finding a sample correlation of such a magnitude if the variables are not really correlated in the population? If the odds are less than five out of a hundred, the finding is said to be statistically significant at the .05 level, the highest probability of chance findings generally accepted by social scientists. A more stringent criterion is the .01 level (only one out of a hundred probability of occurring by chance).

Significance is a factor of both the size of the coefficient and the size of the sample. With small sample sizes the coefficient must be large to be significant because it is riskier to predict a population from a small sample. As sample size grows larger, more certainty is assured, and even small coefficients may be sufficient to infer that *some* relationship exists in the population. In our sample (rather large at 419), a coefficient must reach at least .10 to be significant at the .05 level and at least .13 to be significant at the .01 level.

It is important to remember that when behavioral scientists speak of significant relationships, they mean any relationship that is "real"–that is, different from zero in the population. The actual variance in the one variable that is explained by the second can be determined by squaring the coefficient of correlation. Thus, if intelligence scores and grade-point average are correlated at .50, then intelligence scores account for 25 percent of the variance in grade-point average. A correlation of .20 explains only 4 percent of the variance, and in large samples, even lower correlations may be statistically significant. Why do researchers bother with such apparently small figures? Because human behavior is so complex that no one factor ever explains more than a small portion of any behavior. But through varied research, a body of truth is constructed. It is better to have some truth and insight than none at all.

The Belief Scale was found to be significantly correlated with five public issues: Politics, -.17; Position, -.17; Prayer, -.12; Crime, .10; and Capitalism, .15. Those who expressed stronger agreement with traditional Adventist beliefs were slightly more likely to be against individual Christians and corporate churches becoming involved in political action and to be against a constitutional amendment permitting prayer in public schools. They were more likely to support tougher measures on crime and to uphold capitalism as a Christian ideal. In other words, they leaned toward political conservatism except on the prayer issue where the historic Adventist teaching on separation of church and state no doubt influenced a reversal.

A second look at the data was achieved by dividing the respondents on the Belief scale into two groups–those above and those below the Belief mean (average score). These two groups were compared, in a series of $\underline{t}$-tests, on each of the public issues as well as on an item which read: "Churches should concentrate on proclaiming the gospel and not become involved in trying to change society through social or political action." While this question is actually part of the Religious Maturity scale, it raises social and political themes and, therefore, is used in the $\underline{t}$-tests. It is labeled SocialConcern.

The t-test is a statistical procedure that compares the means or average scores of two groups on a single variable. It asks how likely that the *difference* between the sample means could have occurred if no real difference existed between the two groups in the population. In the present instance, for example, it notes that the high-belief group had a mean of 2.87 (on a scale of 1 to 5) and the low-belief group had a mean of 3.37 on the item Politics. What are the odds that the mean difference of .5 could have occurred by chance if no difference on this item existed in the larger population? The answer? Less than 1 in 1000. So this finding is significant at the .001 level. We won't clutter this chapter by listing all of the various means but will only indicate where significant differences occurred and which group was higher.

In this study the identical five public issues of the correlations proved to be significant and in the same direction. Also, the high-belief group was significantly higher on SocialConcern, indicating that more traditional believers are more likely to agree that churches should concentrate on the Gospel and not become involved in social change. This is in line with their general conservative stance.

Religious Experience

The Experiential Scale was significantly correlated with five public issues: Russia, .13; GovernAid, .11; Position, .13; Crime, .11; and Capitalism, .12. Since all correlations were positive, those whose religion is marked by more subjective experience are more likely to support peaceful relations with the Soviet Union, government aid to minorities, churches becoming involved in political action, tougher measures on crime, and capitalism as a Christian position. The first three are liberal positions; the last two conservative. The lack of consistency explains why there was no correlation between the Experiential and the Public Issues Scales.

Again, high and low experiential groups were formed for a t-test. Of the four significant differences, only two, GovernAid and Capitalism, were the same as the correlations. The two new ones were Racial and Elderly and indicate that those high on experience are more likely to favor the removal of racial restrictions in housing, education, and employment, and to support public insurance for elderly in nursing homes. So this analysis relates subjective experience to three liberal issues and one conservative one–Capitalism.

Chapter 9

Intrinsic-Extrinsic Motivation

The Intrinsic Scale was significantly correlated with only two public issues: Racial, .11 and Capitalism, .11. Those higher on intrinsic orientation are more likely to favor elimination of racial restrictions (the liberal position) and to favor capitalism (the conservative one).

On the t-test, three public issues were found to have significant differences between the groups. Capitalism figures here as before. But high intrinsics are more likely to support government aid to minorities (GovernAid) and to agree that churches should not be active in social concerns (SocialConcern). These last two split on the liberal-conservative continuum.

The three extrinsic items from the Intrinsic Scale were made into an Extrinsic Scale and divided into high and low groups. The six significant differences (SocialConcern, Politics, Position, Prayer, Firearms, and Capitalism) make an interesting mix. Extrinsics favored prayer in public schools, a conservative position. But they also saw both individual Christians and corporate churches becoming involved in politics, favored the registration of firearms, and did not agree that capitalism is connected with Christianity–all liberal stances. These Adventist extrinsics seem to be quite opposite of Adventists who are strong in traditional beliefs.

Religious Maturity

The Religious Maturity Scale was significantly correlated with five public issues: Politics, .20; Position, .13; Prayer, .11; SDI, .10; and SupremeCourt, .11. Those who are more mature in faith (on this scale) approve of individual Christians and corporate churches becoming involved in political action, but they also favor prayer in public schools, Star Wars, and conservative Supreme Court justices.

Five significant differences were discovered between the high and low groups in the maturity t-tests: Politics, Position, Prayer, SupremeCourt, and DeathPenalty. Those high on religious maturity tend to favor involvement in political action by both individual Christians and churches. But they also tend to support prayer in the public schools, conservative Supreme Court justices, and capital punishment.

Church-Related Behaviors

The Church-Related Behaviors Scale was significantly correlated with six public issues: GovernAid, .11; Racial, .13; Prayer, -.20; Contras, .10; UN, .10; and Capitalism, .15. Again, an interesting liberal-conservative mix occurred. Those who engage more frequently in these church-related behaviors are more likely to favor aid to minorities, elimination of racial restrictions, and *not* permitting prayer or Bible reading in public schools. On the other hand, they also favor aid to the Contras, withdrawal from the United Nations, and capitalism as a cousin of Christianity.

In the t-tests, significant differences were found on three variables (SocialConcern, Position, and Prayer), only one of which was the same as for the correlations. In addition to opposing prayer in the public schools, those who engage more frequently in church-related behaviors tend to oppose churches becoming involved in political action and to agree with the social concern item–thus opposing churches working for political and social causes. This presents a consistent conservative stance with the exception of the prayer item, which may be explained by the traditional Adventist separation-of-church-and-state doctrine.

Devotional Practices

The Devotional Scale was correlated significantly with seven public issues: GovernAid, .13; Racial, .15; SupremeCourt, .11; Crime, .11; UN, .11; Firearms, .11; and Capitalism, .15. Those more active in private devotional behavior are more likely to favor government aid to minorities, elimination of racial restrictions, and registration of firearms–all liberal positions. But, they also tend to favor conservative Supreme Court justices, withdrawal from the United Nations, tougher measures on crime, and capitalism–all conservative causes.

The t-tests on devotional practices found only three significant differences: SocialConcern, Prayer, and UN. The public-issue item that is different is Prayer. High devotionals tend to oppose prayer in the public schools even while they tend to favor withdrawal from the United Nations. On SocialConcern they are more likely to agree, thus opposing churches becoming involved in political action.

Religious Imagery

Earlier it was mentioned that because of its extremely low reliability, the Grace scale was not employed in the correlational research. However, a factor analysis revealed that two items (Master-Spouse and Judge-Lover) could form a scale with a respectable reliability. The mean on this new scale was used to divide the sample into high and low groups, and appropriate t-tests were run on the public issues. A significant difference was found only for GovernAid, with Position just on the borderline (probability = .055). Those high on the scale tend to favor government aid to minorities and come very close to being more likely to approve the involvement of churches in political issues.

Salience

In addition to employing the scales, correlational analysis was conducted for three separate religion items: Salience, Foundational World View, and Law. Salience–the measurement of the overall importance of one's faith–was correlated significantly with eight public issues (more than any of the scales): Nuclear, .11; Russia, .19; GovernAid, .15; Racial, .17; Elderly, .14; Crime, .13; Firearms, .12; and Capitalism, .12.

Adventists whose faith is more important to them are more likely to favor nuclear freeze, normal relations with the Soviet Union, aid to minorities, elimination of racial restrictions, nursing-home insurance, and registration of firearms–a liberal agenda by any standard. But they also want tougher measures on crime and perceive capitalism as connected with their religion, so the picture is somewhat confusing.

Foundational World View

Earlier it was mentioned that the three items coded as foundational world view did not make as effective a predictor due to restriction of range resulting from so few Adventists taking a communitarian view. Nevertheless, world view significantly predicted six public issues: Nuclear, .11; GovernAid, .11; Women, .11; Position, .15; Elderly, .10; and Supreme Court, .11. Those who move toward the communitarian (or at least mixed) view are more likely to support nuclear freeze, aid to minorities, ERA, church involvement in political issues, and nursing home insurance. The liberal agenda is broken only by their tendency to favor the appointment of conservative justices to the United States Supreme Court.

Law

In describing the Belief Scale it was mentioned that one item was omitted from the scale because those who agreed with other belief statements tended to agree also with it, even though it did not represent orthodox Adventist theology. The question reads: "A person's standing before God is based on his/her obedience to God's law." This question was found to be significantly correlated with four public issues: Women, .11; Politics, -.14; Prayer, .16; and Crime, .12. It does not seem surprising that law-oriented Adventists would oppose Christians becoming involved in politics or favor prayer in public schools and tougher measures for criminals. It is somewhat unexpected that they tended to favor the Equal Rights Amendment.

Underlying Factors

Another way to view the relationships that have been described so far in this chapter is through a statistical procedure known as factor analysis. When a large group answer a number of items, certain patterns appear. Those who answer certain questions one way tend to answer other questions in a predictable manner. The procedure discovers which items "hang together" and gives that cluster an appropriate name. These are called the "underlying factors."

A factor (principal components) analysis of the eighteen public issues items resulted in five factors. Factor 1–consisting of items on nuclear freeze, Russia, withdrawal from UN (negative), aid to minorities, elimination of racial restrictions, and Equal Rights Amendment–was named "Peace and Justice." Factor 2– made up of defense spending, aid to "Contras," SDI (Star Wars), and conservative justices–was labeled "Defense." Factor 3–composed of items on Christians and churches becoming involved in political action and churches sticking to preaching the gospel (negative)–was called "Political Involvement." Factor 4–comprising crime control, capital punishment, and capitalism–was named "Law and Order." Factor 5 was somewhat of a mixed bag (prayer amendment, nursing home insurance, and registration of firearms) that we labeled "Government Intervention."

The religion variables were also submitted to a principal components analysis which resulted in six interpretable factors. Factor 1 contained the three items on the experiential dimension plus the seven intrinsic items from Hoge's scale. It has been labeled "Relationship with God." Factor 2 combines the church-related behavior and the devotional items and has been named "Religious Practice." Factor 3 combines the six orthodoxy or belief items with two items from the Religious Maturity Scale which were intended to indicate immaturity. We called it "Orthodoxy." Factor 4 draws on items from the Religious Maturity Scale which were intended to measure Allport's sense of tentativeness, humility, and heuristic qualities. It has been labeled "Openness to Change." Factor 5 employed the three extrinsic items from Hoge's scale as well as the measure of Foundational World View and has been named "Extrinsic." Finally, Factor 6 was made up of three of the four items from Greeley's scale and has been named "Grace."

Next, we calculated correlations between each public issues factor and each religion factor. We found that for Factor 1, Peace and Justice, only Openness to Change of the religion factors was correlated significantly, and the relationship was weak (.11). Those less dogmatic in their faith are somewhat more likely to favor positions supporting international peace and social justice for minorities and women.

Openness to Change was also the only religion factor significantly correlated with Factor 2, Defense (.15). In this sample those more open to religious ideas tended to support policies that would strengthen national defense.

Religion proved to be a better predictor of Factor 3, Political Involvement. Three of the religion factors were significantly correlated with it: Orthodoxy (-.36), Religious Practice (-.16), and Openness to Change (.15). The negative relationship with Orthodoxy was particularly strong for this study.

Those who are closest to traditional belief and who practice their religion most faithfully are most likely to oppose corporate churches and individual Christians becoming involved in political action. Those who are less dogmatic and more open to change tend to favor such action.

The only religion factor significantly correlated with Factor 4, Law and Order, was Openness to Change (.14), although Orthodoxy was close (.08). That the more flexible and less dogmatic should tend toward stricter law enforcement and favor capitalism is somewhat puzzling since it seems to go opposite to the theory. The near hit for Orthodoxy would have been more along the expected lines.

Factor 5, Government Intervention, was significantly correlated with three religion factors: Extrinsic (.25), Relationship with God (.13), and Religious Practice (-.12). Government Intervention tends to be favored by those higher on the Extrinsic and Relationship with God factors and opposed by those more diligent in the practice of their religion. Since Government Intervention contains two clearly liberal items (firearms registration and nursing home insurance) and a conservative item likely to be opposed by conservative Adventists (prayer amendment) because of Adventism's position on church and state, a high score on this factor would seem to indicate liberal politics. Adventists, then, who are extrinsic or experiential in their religion may lean toward liberal issues while those who adhere most faithfully to church-related behaviors and devotional practices are likely to favor conservative politics.

Political Party

Moving from public issues themselves, we now turn to political identification as revealed by political party preference, political orientation, and voting behavior. Profiles of religious responses were created for each of these choices. Items where the percentage points differed to any extent were selected and made into three charts–one for each of the questions.

The first chart contrasts Democrats with Republicans. In cases where the question calls for a response of disagree-agree, the percentages listed are the total of those choosing responses "somewhat agree" or "strongly agree." For other questions, the selection information is included. Items are listed only if the groups are separated by at least ten percentage points.

Statement	Democrat	Republican
Certain of a conversion experience	89%	79%
Could be mistaken on some points of religion	52%	67%
Struggled to understand problems of evil, suffering, and death	70%	58%
Study the Bible regularly	8%	77%

Ten or more points separate the two parties on four religious items. Democrats were more likely to claim a conversion experience, struggle with the problem of evil, and engage in regular Bible study and less likely to recognize that they might be mistaken on some points of their religion.

In addition to separating the groups on individual items, we also used Analysis of Variance (ANOVA) to determine if significant differences occurred on the scales. Democrats were higher on the Experiential Scale than Independents, Repub-licans, or those with no interest in politics, suggesting that they are more likely to experience religion subjectively. Democrats were also higher than either Independents or those with no interest in politics on the Intrinsic Scale, suggesting that their faith is more important to them.

While not significantly higher than Republicans, Democrats were the highest of any group on the Salience measure–significantly higher than those who had no interest in politics on the importance of their faith. Democrats were also significantly higher than Independents on the Belief Scale. On the Extrinsic Scale, Republicans were lower than all other categories.

Of course, we are not suggesting that being Democrat or Republican *causes* these differences. It may be that these characteristics influenced choice of a political party. Or a background variable may have influenced both party identification and religious variations. For example, we noted in chapter 7 that Blacks were higher on the Experiential Scale than Whites. And Blacks are more likely to identify with the Democratic party. Thus, the fact that Democrats are likely to be higher on religious experience than

Republicans may be at least partly explained by the ethnicity variable.

Political Orientation

Since so few Adventists identified themselves as "liberals," we combined these with the "moderates" and contrasted this combination with "conservatives." The chart shows differences of at least ten percentage points.

Statement	Conservative	Moderate Liberal
Churches preach gospel/ avoid politics	74%	60%
Can't be sure of all truth but worth acting on anyway	54%	67%
Religious beliefs same as 5 years ago	74%	60%
Have regular family worship	61%	47%
Our Firm Foundation is valuable	17%	5%

On the religious questions, conservatives were more likely to want churches to stay out of politics, to have the same religious beliefs they had five years previously, to engage in regular family worship, and to value *Our Firm Foundation*. They were less likely to be willing to act on a belief about which they could not be absolutely certain.

On the scales, liberals (few though they were) were significantly more likely to lean toward a communitarian world view than conservatives, moderates, or those with no political opinions. Those of no opinion and conservatives were significantly more orthodox than the liberals, and those of no opinion were more orthodox than the moderates. Liberals and moderates ranked significantly higher on the Religious Maturity Scale than did those of no opinion. Conservatives were more involved in church-related behaviors than moderates or liberals. All of this is in harmony with the theoretical framework, including the hypothesis that those most traditional in belief are most likely to avoid politics.

Recent Voting Behavior

The following chart shows the contrasts among those who voted for Reagan in 1984, voted for Mondale, or didn't vote. Differences on the religious questions of at least ten points between any two groups are given.

Statement	Reagan	Mondale	No vote
Second Advent in our generation	56%	60%	69%
Feel close to God in worship	85%	95%	91%
Prepared to alter religious beliefs with new light	60%	50%	53%
Could be mistaken on some points of religion	71%	48%	81%

Chapter 9

Faith, a developmental process	89%	92%	81%
Struggled to understand problems of evil and suffering	57%	68%	59%
Churches preach gospel/ avoid political action	71%	49%	73%
Not dogmatic about religion	55%	44%	42%
Beliefs same as 5 years ago	75%	59%	63%
Hold a church office	38%	37%	50%
Pray privately regularly	81%	90%	93%
Picture God as Father	69%	59%	69%
Picture God as King	38%	45%	34%

Mondale supporters were more likely to feel close to God than those who voted for Reagan. Reaganites were more open than supporters of Mondale to alter their religious beliefs, more likely to admit they could be mistaken, less likely to have struggled with the problems of evil, much more likely to want the church to stay out of politics, more hesitant to be dogmatic, and less likely to have actually changed their beliefs over the past five years. They tended to pray less and to picture God more as a father.

Those who didn't vote in 1984 were more likely than Reagan supporters to believe that Jesus Christ will come in this generation and more likely to pray regularly and less hesitant to be dogmatic in their religious assertions. They were more likely than Reaganites to have changed their religious beliefs to some extent over the past five years.

Nonvoters were less likely than supporters of Mondale to view faith as a developmental process or to conceive of God as King. They were more likely to picture God as Father than those who voted for Mondale and much more likely to want the church to stay out of politics. They were more likely than either of the two groups of voters to recognize that they could be mistaken on some points in their religion and to hold a church office.

The ANOVA for the scales shows that those who voted for either Mondale or Reagan were more likely to espouse a communitarian world view than those who did not vote. Voting in itself, regardless of the candidate, shows some willingness to engage in the improvement of society. Those who voted for Reagan were significantly higher on the Religious Maturity Scale than either of the other groups, and those who voted for Mondale were higher on the Experiential scale than those who voted for Reagan.

Thus analysis of religion with political party preference, political orientation, and recent voting behavior presents a mixed picture. Some findings square neatly with the theoretical framework, but others do not. Most helpful of the three measures in constructing an explanatory framework is political orientation where the findings fit the theory very well.

Political party does not prove to be as consistent. Although a far greater percentage of moderates/liberals than conservatives identified themselves as Democrats (34% to 12%), and a far smaller percentage of moderates/liberals than conservatives identified themselves as Republicans (38% to 64%), yet the alignment of Republicans with conservatives and moderate/liberals with Democrats is far from perfect. This is illustrated by the fact that more moderates/liberals identified themselves as Republicans than Democrats (38% to 34%). This no doubt reflects the overall tendency of Adventists to be Republicans and indicates that the "moderate"

Adventist might well be a conservative in some other camp.

Voting behavior proves to be even more inconsistent a predictor in the theoretical framework. While moderates/liberals were more likely to vote for Mondale than conservatives were (26% to 7%) and less likely than conservatives to vote for Reagan (45% to 63%), yet the correspondence between political orientation and voting was generally weak. This can be seen by the fact that while nearly all voting conservatives cast their ballots for Reagan (63% compared to 7% for Mondale), nearly twice as many moderates/liberals voted for Reagan as they did for Mondale (45% to 26%). Thus, it is difficult to fit party identification and voting for Reagan into the conservative-liberal political continuum–at least among Seventh-day Adventists.

Journal Readership

Earlier it was noted that the great majority of the sample had no familiarity with any of the journals listed, and, therefore, these periodicals were not of great value in the analysis. Still, we selected two of the journals for a quick look. *Our Firm Foundation* and *Spectrum* are the two best-known journals on the list and represent opposite ends of the Adventist theological continuum. For each journal, two groups were selected–those who found it of little worth and those who found it valuable. Differences between the groups are shown for each political question where they equal or exceed ten percentage points. The percentages given represent those who favor the issue or who are classified in the particular political group. It must be kept in mind that these charts are based on only a small fraction of the sample, so one should not make too much of these differences. Nevertheless, they do provide a perspective. It must also be emphasized that no comparison is made between the two journals–only between the way two different groups react to each one.

Our Firm Foundation

Political Item	Little Worth	Valuable
Freeze on nuclear weapons	72%	59%
Equal Rights Amendment	69%	45%
Christians involved in politics	45%	26%
Churches involved in political action	22%	10%
Conservative Supreme Court justices	22%	12%
Registration of firearms	40%	63%
Identify with Democrats	32%	18%
Did not vote in 1984	40%	51%
Conservative orientation	38%	49%
Moderate orientation	30%	18%
Liberal orientation	20%	0%
No political opinions	13%	33%

On the six public issues that show a difference, the "valuable" group took the more conservative position on four, but were less likely to favor conservative justices and more likely to favor gun control. The latter position may result from orthodox Adventist opposition to violence and a strong regard for the commandment that reads: "Thou shalt not kill." The Supreme Court item is more difficult to harmonize.

Those who find the journal valuable are less likely to be Democrats and more likely to have a conservative political orientation or no opinion (none are liberals) and not to have voted at all in 1984. Thus, esteem for this journal is a fairly good predictor of conservative political opinions, though it must be emphasized that the numbers are too small to provide significant results.

Spectrum

Political Item	Little Worth	Valuable
Government aid to improve minorities lot	57%	38%
Elimination of all racial restrictions	89%	79%
Equal Rights Amendment	69%	54%
Christians involved in politic	67%	38%
Control crime with tougher laws	71%	81%
Registration of firearms	72%	52%
Identify with Democrats	13%	31%
No political identification	17%	5%
Voted for Mondale in 1984	6%	15%
Did not vote in 1984	43%	28%
Conservative orientation	37%	23%
Liberal orientation	6%	15%

On the six public issues showing at least a ten-point difference, those who find *Spectrum* valuable were more conservative on every one–a surprising finding, given the liberal reputation of the journal. Yet they were more likely to be Democrats, to have voted for Mondale, and to identify themselves as political liberals and less likely to see themselves as conservatives. Their attitudes toward public issues do not seem to match their political self-identification or their voting behavior. But the small numbers may make this finding unreliable.

Attempting to integrate the varying findings of this chapter into some unifying framework is not easy. However, we "make a stab" at it in chapter 11 for we need to know what all of this means. The picture is too complicated to grasp clearly, and we need to simplify it by reducing it to several easily understood constructs. But first, we must consider some other variables which may well intervene between religion and politics.

Chapter 10

Social Sources of Political Position

A survey researcher with a bent for the unusual might discover a strong positive correlation between the number of sailboats each day on Lake Michigan and the daily volume of popsicle sales on the streets of Chicago. In spite of the established significant relationship, however, such a researcher would not likely conclude that selling popsicles caused sailboats to appear on the Lake or that the presence of billowing sails influenced people to rush to the nearest ice cream dealer. He/she would more correctly deduce that a third variable was having an impact on both sailing and selling–in this case, average daily temperature.

Social scientists like to warn that "correlation does not prove causation." Even if two variables can be demonstrated to be highly related, that fact does not prove that one causes the other, as tobacco companies like to argue (somewhat unsuccessfully in this case) concerning cigarette smoking and lung cancer. Other intervening variables could be involved.

In the case of religion and politics, Niebuhr suggested more than sixty years ago that an important intervening variable was social class.[1] People in lower socioeconomic classes tend to join different religious groups than those of higher status do, and the expression of their faith in social and political attitudes and behaviors tends to be different.

Of course, Niebuhr was talking about *denominations*. Lower classes, for example, tend to be over-represented in Pentecostal churches, and upper classes tend to be over-represented in the Episcopal church. But even within a single denomination–like Seventh-day Adventism–social class may determine to some extent with which local congregation a member affiliates, and it certainly may affect how members translate their faith into positions and actions in the public arena.

To test out this hypothesis, we included eleven demographic variables on our questionnaire. Demographic questions are used to collect the type of personal information which allows researchers to classify people into groups that are useful for social research. The United States Census, for example, is almost entirely composed of demographic questions.

We used gender, length of time as an Adventist, Adventist background, marital status, age, ethnicity, income, education, and years in Adventist schools on the elementary, secondary, and college levels. Income and education are standard ways to determine social class; and gender, marital status, age, and ethnicity are commonly used classifications. The other five variables relate uniquely to groupings of Adventists. First, we present a picture of how our sample–intended to be representative of all adult Adventists in the United States (but actually under representing Blacks and Hispanics)–fits into these demographic patterns. Then we note how these variables relate to attitudes toward public issues.

Social Characteristics of American Adventists

Approximately 41 percent of our sample was male, with the remaining 59 percent female. Dozens of studies of various church congregations in the United States conducted by the Institute of Church Ministry over the last decade agree that the American church is 55 percent to 60 percent female.

The marital status of our sample was as follows:

Presently married	66%
Never married	11%
Separated or divorced	11%
Widowed	12%

This list indicates that approximately one-third of American Adventist adults are not currently married. The proportion of single Adventists may well be even higher for at least two reasons. First, only members eighteen years of age and older were included in the sample, and we may assume that most members under eighteen are unmarried. Second, in a household where both married and single Adventists resided, it is somewhat more likely that a married member would be the one to complete the survey form.

In passing, we note that we may not conclude that "only" 11 percent of Adventist homes have been broken by divorce since an unknown proportion of those who are presently married may have previously divorced and then later remarried.

We classified the age of our respondents into the following groups:

19 years or less	2%
20-35 years	26%
36-50 years	24%
51-65 years	23%
Over 65 years	25%

We would not expect a large number in the first group, given that the minimum age for inclusion in the sample was 18 years. The other groups were quite evenly distributed, but cause for concern is found in the fact that nearly half of the members were over fifty, and a fourth were of retirement age. A church poised for growth would have greater proportions in the 20-to-50-year range.

The ethnic breakdown was as follows:

Asian	2%
Black	10%
Hispanic	3%
White	82%
Other	3%

Whites were obviously over-represented in this sample. While no exact ethnic count has ever been made of the entire church, projections by the North American Division indicate that the membership in North America is 3 percent Asian, 25 percent Black, 8 percent Hispanic, and 64 percent White. The under-representation of Blacks and Hispanics is at least partially explained by the lower response rates of minorities to mail surveys typically found in social science research. This means that when the data from this study are examined as a whole, they may not accurately reflect the picture among Blacks and Hispanics. For a more complete discussion of the limitations of these data, see the appendix.

Income and education taken together constitute a fair measure of socioeconomic status. Yearly family income in this sample was as follows:

Under $10,000	16%
$10,000 to $15,999	18%
$16,000 to $24,999	22%
$25,000 to $49,999	32%
$50,000 or over	12%

Family income was quite evenly distributed across the categories except that a somewhat larger proportion fell into the category between $25,000 and $50,000. American Adventists come from all social strata, but few are really wealthy. The educational level of the sample tended to be somewhat higher than that of the nation at large, however, with 67 percent having gone to college and nearly a third holding at least a four-year degree. For example, the Valuegenesis study found that 66 percent of the graduates from Adventist academies enter college compared with 30 percent from public high schools.[2]

Less than 7th grade completed	2%
Finished 7th to 9th grade	7%
Finished 10th or 11th grade	7%
Graduated from high school	17%
Some college training	36%
Four-year college graduate	18%
Graduate degree (M.A., Ph.D., etc.)	13%

The remaining five demographics examine Adventist backgrounds. In order to determine if a respondent was raised in an Adventist home, we asked: "Was at least one of your parents an Adventist sometime during the first 12 years of your life?" The sample was fairly evenly divided with 54 percent having had at least one Adventist parent and 46 percent having been reared in a non-Adventist home. We also asked the number of years that the respondents had been baptized members of the Adventist church.

Less than 1 year	2%
1 to 5 years	9%
6 to 10 years	9%
11 to 20 years	20%
Over 20 years	60%

The heavy concentration of those who have been members over twenty years is typical of what other recent unpublished studies by the Institute of Church Ministry drawn from Adventist household lists have found and, taken with the age groupings (about half over 50 years old), suggest an aging church in the United States–at least among the Whites.[3] This finding also is not good news for the church's outreach. Church-growth studies have shown that new converts have the greatest network of unchurched friends and relatives to whom they may witness and, consequently, make the most effective soul winners.[4] By the time people have been Adventists for twenty years, they may have few close contacts outside the church.

Only about 40 percent of our sample had secured any of their formal education in Adventist schools at any level. For example, 61 percent had never attended Adventist elementary schools, while 21 percent had attended all eight grades. The others were quite evenly distributed between 1 and 7 years. On the secondary level, 59 percent had never attended an Adventist academy, while 26 percent had gone all four years. Finally, 59 percent had not attended Adventist colleges, while 13 percent had attended four years and another 7 percent had spent five to seven years in these institutions of higher learning.

Demographics and Public Issues

Next, we must ask the question: Do the different demographic variables predict positions on public issues? Seven of the demographic questions collected data on an ordinal level (years of church membership, age, income, education, and years in Adventist elementary, secondary, and college schools). The ordinal level of measurement means that the various responses are organized on an ascending scale. For example, being 20-35 years old is higher than being 19 years or fewer, and an income of $50,000 is more than one of $25,000. Correlations between these variables and the public issues were examined for significance. The remaining four demographic questions (gender, Adventist background, marital status, and ethnicity) are at the nominal level of measurement. The responses are only labels or names and do not represent an ascending scale. For example, being male is not higher than being female and Hispanic is not up the scale from Black, even though Black is choice #2 and Hispanic is choice #3. These four variables were examined by analysis of variance, including range tests.

Years of Church Membership

The item "years as a member" allows for five ascending classifications for the number of years the respondents have been baptized Adventists. This variable was significantly correlated with only one public issue–Prayer (-.16). Those longer in the church were more likely to oppose a constitutional amendment to permit prayer and/or Bible reading in public schools. This finding is quite consistent with the theory that has been presented. The longer one is socialized into the Adventist church, the more one internalizes into the belief system the notion of separating church and state.

Age grouping was significantly correlated with three public issues–Racial (-.14), Prayer (-.13), and Contras (-.16). Those who are older tended to oppose elimination of all racial restrictions, prayer in public schools, and military aid to the Contras. The first issue is conservative, and while the latter two are usually considered liberal causes, the Adventist positions on separation of church and state and noncombatancy may provide a consistency for this set.

Family Income

Yearly family income was significantly correlated with eight public issues–GovernAid (-.15), Racial (.20), Politics (.19), Defense (.12), Contras (.23), SupremeCourt (.23), Capitalism (.12), and DeathPenalty (.17). Those with higher incomes were more likely to oppose government aid to minorities and to favor elimination of racial restrictions, individual Christians becoming involved in political action, increased spending for national defense, military aid to the Contras, conservative Supreme Court justices, capitalism as being in harmony with Biblical Christianity, and capital punishment. Six of the eight are conservative positions. Those who are better off seek to preserve the status quo by giving religious legitimation to capitalism and opposing systems that propose some distribution of the wealth.

Level of Education

Years of formal education was significantly correlated with eight public issues–Nuclear (.12); Racial (.24); Politics (.23); Position (.12); Defense (.17); Contras (.14); SupremeCourt (.17); and DeathPenalty (.12). Those who have more formal education tended to favor a nuclear freeze, elimination of racial restrictions, both individual Christians and corporate churches becoming involved in political action, increased spending for national defense, military aid to the Contras, conservative justices, and capital punishment. While the first four are liberal positions–expected to correlate with higher educational attainments–the last four are conservative positions that go contrary to the theory that social liberalism and education are positively related. Adventists seem to vary from the norm here.

Adventist Elementary Schools

Years in attendance at Adventist elementary schools was significantly correlated with two public issues–Crime (.10) and DeathPenalty (.19). Those who have spent more years in Adventist elementary schools were more likely to support tougher measures to control crime, including capital punishment. Perhaps Adventist schools tend to foster a law orientation.

Adventist Secondary Schools

Years in attendance at Adventist secondary schools was significantly correlated with four public issues– GovernAid (-.16); Contras (.14); SupremeCourt (.11); and DeathPenalty (.20). Those who have attended Adventist academies longer tended to oppose government aid for minorities and to favor military aid to the Contras, conservative justices on the U.S. Supreme Court, and capital punishment. So attendance at Adventist elementary and secondary schools tends to predict–where it predicts at all–a conservative socio-political posture.

Adventist Colleges

Years in attendance at Adventist colleges or universities was significantly correlated with five public issues–Racial (.11); Politics (.12); SupremeCourt (.11); UN (-.11); and DeathPenalty (.11). Those with more Adventist college education were more likely to favor elimination of racial restrictions, individual Christians becoming involved in political action, conservative Supreme Court justices, and capital punishment. They are more likely to oppose withdrawal of the United States from the United Nations organization. Thus, they present a mixed picture as to liberal and conservative positions.

The remaining four demographic variables were analyzed by analysis of variance (ANOVA). This procedure determines whether or not at least one significant difference between the various groups occurred. The categories under each were used as the groups, and the public-issues statements constituted the continuous dependent variables. Only those analyses significant at the .05 level or beyond are mentioned. If a significant finding occurred in an item with more than two categories (marital status and ethnicity), range tests indicate where the significant differences lie.

Gender

A significant difference between genders was found on the following public issues:

Public Issue	Male Mean	Female Mean	Prob
Nuclear	4.19	3.90	.03
Racial	4.44	4.10	.01
Defense	2.61	2.25	.01
Contras	2.73	2.28	.001
UN	2.32	2.05	.05
Capitalism	3.79	3.19	.001
DeathPenalty	3.86	3.55	.001

In each of these seven significant differences, the males had the higher mean. Men are more likely than women to favor a nuclear freeze, elimination of racial restrictions, increased spending for national defense, military aid to the Contras, withdrawal from the United Nations, capitalism as being compatible with Christianity, and capital punishment. With the exception of the first two, males seem to take a more conservative political stance.

Adventist Background

This item serves as a rough measure of whether subjects were reared in Adventist homes or became members following their childhood. A significant difference between the two groups was found on the following public issues:

Public Issue	SDAChild	SDAAdult	Prob
Russia	4.31	4.08	.05
Contras	2.60	2.32	.04

This variable did not discriminate well. In the two differences, those brought up in Adventist homes were more likely to favor peaceful relations with Russia and aid to the Contras than were those who became Adventists later. While this seems contradictory, an inspection of the means indicates that the majority of both groups tended to favor the first issue and oppose the second.

Marital Status

Respondents were grouped according to this question as presently married, never married, separated/divorced, or widowed. Significant differences among these groups were discovered by ANOVA for six public issues.

Public Issue	Married	Single	Divorced	Widowed	Prob
GovernAid	3.17	3.93	3.59	3.48	.01
Racial	4.26	4.74	4.39	3.64	.001
Contras	2.58	2.52	2.57	1.70	.001
SupremeCourt	2.71	2.52	2.59	2.08	.02
Crime	4.24	3.89	4.26	3.78	.04
DeathPenalty	3.72	3.43	3.59	2.82	.01

On GovernAid, only the difference between married and single is significant with the single having been more likely to favor government aid to minorities.

On Racial, the single were more likely to favor the elimination of all racial restrictions than the married were, and the widowed were more likely to oppose it than each of the other groups.

On Contras, the widowed were more likely to oppose military aid to the Contras than each of the other groups were.

On SupremeCourt, the married were more likely to favor the appointment of conservative justices than the widowed were.

On Crime, the married were more likely to favor tougher measures to deal with crime than the widows were.

On DeathPenalty, the widowed were more likely to oppose capital punishment than were the married and the divorced.

Ethnic Background

Respondents were grouped according to this question as Asian, Black, Hispanic, White, and Other. Significant differences among these groups were discovered by ANOVA for seven public issues.

Public Issue	Asian	Black	Hispanic	White	Other	Prob
GovernAid	3.50	4.27	3.69	3.19	4.00	.001
Prayer	3.60	3.05	3.08	2.64	4.46	.001
Contras	2.40	2.27	3.46	2.49	1.77	.02
Elderly	4.30	4.44	4.15	3.91	4.54	.02
Firearms	4.00	4.49	3.46	3.62	3.69	.02
Capitalism	4.30	3.44	2.38	3.50	2.31	.001
DeathPenalty	3.80	2.44	2.85	3.73	3.38	.001

On GovernAid, Blacks and Others were more likely to favor government aid to minorities than were Whites.

On Prayer, Others were more likely to favor prayer or Bible reading in public schools than Blacks, Hispanics or Whites were.

On Contras, Hispanics were more likely to favor military aid than Blacks, Whites, or Others were.

On Elderly, Blacks were more likely to favor government insurance for nursing homes than Whites were.

On Firearms, Blacks were more likely to support gun registration than either Whites or Hispanics were.

On Capitalism, both Hispanics and Others were more likely to oppose the concept that capitalism harmonizes with Biblical Christianity than were Asians, Blacks, or Whites.

On DeathPenalty, Asians were more likely than Blacks, and Whites were more likely than either Blacks or Hispanics to favor capital punishment.

Thus demographic variables do account for some of the variance in attitudes toward public issues but by no means for all of it. To what extent do they explain the relationships between religion and politics?

Controlling for Demographic Variables

In chapter 9 we reported on the use of underlying factors as a means of relating religion and politics. We discovered five political factors and sought correlations between them and six religion factors. Those correlations that were significant were listed and discussed.

In this chapter we go a bit farther and ask: If the demographic variables were first allowed to explain all the variance in the political factors that they could, would significant explanatory power still be left for the religion factors? Another way to ask this question is: Do the religion variables provide any influence on political attitudes beyond what is already provided by the various demographic groupings? This is called *controlling for demographics.*

While a number of possible means may be used to achieve this end, we employed multiple-regression analysis. This procedure allows the correlation of one dependent variable (here a political factor) with a *combination* of independent variables (religion factors and demographic variables). More than that, it removes any overlapping variance from the independent variables that occurs from their being correlated with each other so that it can be determined what the unique influence of a particular variable is on the dependent variable in the presence of all the other independent variables.

The combination of independent variables forms a mathematical equation. Using a stepwise procedure, variables can be introduced into the equation one by one. The first one entered is the one that makes the greatest contribution to explaining the variance of the dependent variable–thus the most important. The process continues until no unentered variable can make a further significant contribution to the equation.

In chapter 9 we introduced only religion factors into the equation. Here we also introduced the demographic variables. If a religion factor was significantly correlated with a political factor *only* because they were both correlated with a demographic variable, the demographic will be retained in the equation and the religion factor eliminated. However, if the religion factor has explanatory power independently of the demographic variable, it will still be significant in the equation. Thus, we control for the demographics.

In order to use nominal measurements in regression analysis, it is necessary to transform them to an ordinal level. This is no problem for variables with only two choices since the up and down can be easily interpreted. For example, if 1 = male and 2 = female, then we know that positive correlations mean females are more likely to have the quality being measured and negative correlations mean males are more likely to possess it. For three or more choices, however, the results are not interpretable. Therefore, we coded the marital status variable to just two classes–"married" and "not married," and the ethnicity variable to "white" and "minority."

For Factor 1, Peace and Justice, one may recall, of the religion factors only Openness to Change was significant. Those less dogmatic in their faith were somewhat more likely to favor positions supporting international peace and social justice for minorities and women. None of the demographic variables was significant. Thus the weak relationship between Peace and Justice and Openness to Change cannot be accounted for by the background variables.

Openness to Change was also the only religion factor significant for Factor 2, Defense. Surprisingly, those who were more tentative about their religion tended to favor defense items. Again, the background variables were not significant. Thus demographics do not wash out this rather odd relationship.

Religion proved to be a better predictor of Factor 3, Political Involvement. A regression of all the religion factors and demographic variables on Political Involvement yielded a multiple correlation of .47, highly significant at .001. Only three of the factors–Orthodoxy, Religious Practice, and Openness to Change–however, contributed significantly to the relationship, with Orthodoxy making a particularly strong negative contribution (-.36). Those who are closest to traditional belief and who practice their religion most faithfully were most likely to oppose corporate churches and individual Christians becoming involved in political action. Those who are less dogmatic and more open to change tended to favor such action.

Two of the background variables were also significant contributors to this equation–education and gender. Those with higher levels of formal education and females tended to be more favorable toward political involvement.

However, the three religion factors continued to make a significant contribution in the presence of education and gender, so the relationship between these factors and political involvement cannot be explained entirely by these demographic characteristics.

For Factor 4, Law and Order, only Openness to Change had a significant correlation, although Orthodoxy was borderline. The more flexible and less dogmatic members tended toward stricter law enforcement and were more likely to favor capitalism. Most of this variance, however was explained by two background variables–ethnicity and years as an Adventist. Whites were more favorable than minorities toward the Law and Order issues, and those who have been in the church longer (perhaps a proxy for age) were more likely to favor them than were the newer converts. Openness to Change was weakened by the demographics, but still retained some influence on Law and Order.

The regression on Factor 5, Government Intervention, yielded a multiple correlation of .43, with Extrinsic and Religious Practice still making significant contributions in the presence of five demographic variables–family income, years as Adventist, ethnicity, gender, and level of education. Government intervention tended to be favored by those higher on the Extrinsic factor and opposed by those more diligent in the practice of their religion. Adventists, then, who are extrinsic in their religion may lean toward liberal issues while those who adhere most faithfully to ritual and devotional practices are likely to favor conservative politics.

For the demographics, minorities and women were more likely to favor such intervention than Whites or males were. Those with less education, less income, and fewer years as Adventists were also more likely to be favorable. Before the introduction of these background variables, Relationship with God had been a significant predictor of Government Intervention along with Extrinsic and Religious Practice. In the presence of the five demographic variables, Relationship with God is no longer significant, which means that once ethnicity and gender are taken into consideration, experiential religion no longer has an impact on attitudes toward government intervention. The influence of Extrinsicness and Religious Practice, however, is not completely accounted for by the background variables.

Thus we conclude that while certain demographic variables–especially ethnicity, education, age, and gender–are related to attitudes on public issues, in most cases their influence does not weaken that of certain religion factors to the point of non-significance. While the effect of religion on political views is by no means strong, it does exist, to some extent, independent of that of demographic considerations.

References

[1] H. Richard Niebuhr, *The Social Sources of Denominationalism* (New York: Henry Holt, 1929).

[2] Project Affirmation, "Valuegenesis: A Project Affirmation Study of the Influence of Family, School, and Church on the Formation of Faith," unpublished data analyses (available at the North American Division Office of Education, Silver

Spring, MD); Roger L. Dudley, *Valuegenesis: Faith in the Balance* (Riverside, CA: La Sierra University Press, 1992).

³Roger L. Dudley and Des Cummings, Jr., *Adventures in Church Growth* (Hagerstown, MD: Review and Herald Publishing Association, 1983), 51-57.

⁴C. Peter Wagner, *Your Church Can Grow* (Glendale, CA: Regal Books, 1976).

Chapter 11

Making Sense Out of It All

In the previous chapters of this book, we have presented many findings from this research study, and we have tried to interpret these findings in the light of a theoretical framework and in the context of the history of Seventh-day Adventism in the United States. We have discovered that most of the findings do make sense when seen through the filter of theory and history, but that a few pieces of the puzzle do not appear to fit into a harmonious pattern as we perceive it. Drawing on consistency theory, we have affirmed that if we could only see things from the viewpoint of a particular respondent, his or her positions would seem consistent, and cognitive dissonance would be reduced.

All of this seems somewhat fragmented and scattered throughout the various chapters, however. In this chapter we attempt to pull it together and annunciate several broad themes that seem implicit in this morass of data. We do not venture to repeat all the detailed explanations of the foregoing chapters. The reader is referred back to them for more detail, but we do look for the larger picture–what all of this means.

Church as a Political Community

Churches are groups which socialize their members not only to conform to religious beliefs and behaviors but also to political positions. Not that most churches take an overt political position (although some do). But multiple avenues exist whereby political messages can be communicated in a religious group setting. The network associations with people of common background and social status reinforce a sense of group awareness. The role of Christian education both in its parochial school system and through the Sabbath school is a powerful avenue for the transmission of norms and values. The minister is also a source for political cues. As the spiritual leader, the minister becomes a primary transmitter, be it through homilies, teaching, or personal influence, of the role of religion in secular life. Through these and other avenues, the church tends to create commitments to certain norms of belief and behavior.[1]

It is very likely that these norms may include messages with specific political outlooks, or they may merely communicate those ideological elements that may lead towards the development of political perspectives, such as theological assumptions, a sense of social status, and group interests. Through these multiple cues, churches may reinforce the political differences that exist between denominations.[2] Thus, while individual congregations may, and do, differ somewhat, the general theology and historical experience of Adventists inclines them in general toward a certain stance in the public arena that distinguishes them from other denominations.

How then do differences between individuals within the church arise? We have noted that background variables such as age, education, and ethnicity explain part of this variation. But to the extent that religion stands independent of these demographics as a predictor of political attitudes and behaviors, we must look to the degree of commitment to the teachings and practices of the church. People may be formal members of a religious organization without becoming ritually involved in church life while other members are highly involved. Various levels of agreement with the teachings of the denomination may be found. For those with minimal or no commitment, political attitudes and behaviors are forged apart from church norms, whereas the highly committed are more likely to accept the dominant political message of the group.[3]

Chapter 11

Orthodoxy and Political Stance

With this in mind, we note that Adventists who are most committed to the traditional teachings of the church are likely to be found taking one of two possible stances. Either they hold conservative political positions, or they withdraw from politics completely. The findings for orthodoxy are stronger than for any other measure of religion, and the above conclusion was supported across the board except, as noted, for ethnic minorities.

The ideologically committed are likely to take conservative political positions, first of all, because they have a mind set that wants to preserve the status quo. Their text may well be: "Ask for the old paths, where is the good way, and walk therein" (Jeremiah 6:16). Conservative people feel threatened by change since it upsets the equilibrium and disturbs their comfortable position. If something has proved its worth, "Why change now?" they may ask. Thus, they are likely to support the present capitalistic system and its social arrangements and to favor measures that would defend it from internal and external enemies. They are also likely to want to preserve long-accepted values, especially those that revolve around traditional family structures such as breadwinning father, homemaking mother, and obedient children. Since those high on orthodoxy tend to put much emphasis on the law of God–and by extension, law in general–they are more likely to favor law-and-order issues such as tougher penalties for crimes and capital punishment.

The strongly orthodox also are committed to an eschatological solution to the evil in the world. The answer to societal problems is found in the second coming of Christ, the cataclysmic destruction of contemporary culture, and the creation of a new earth wherein dwells righteousness. Thus they see social action programs as only bandaids for a terminally ill society. Working for social justice appears to be only a diversion from proclaiming the Gospel that would prepare individuals for the new age. As a consequence, they are more likely to oppose the church and individual Adventists becoming involved in the political process. Given the church's teaching that all humans are children of the heavenly Father, they generally favor removing racial restrictions and allowing equal opportunity for all. But they are not much for providing aid to achieve that equality in line with their self-help theology of individual salvation. In their view the church should concentrate on saving sinners, not society.

Since the strongly orthodox are likely to be committed to the "great controversy" view of history, they tend to see Satan working everywhere to attempt to overthrow God's government. This may foster "conspiracy theories" which would see communism or Catholicism as sinister forces attempting to destroy God's work and oppose God's people. Therefore, the orthodox may tend toward anticommunism and pro-capitalism. They may also perceive the conspiracy in scientific evolution, secular humanism, and Biblical criticism and thus favor measures to restrain these movements and preserve more Bible-supported values.

On the other hand, those not as firmly committed to orthodox teachings–presumably those with more exposure to functional rationalization and cultural pluralism–are more open to the possibility of change. While they do not necessarily deny the Adventist eschatological scenario and the presence of conspiracies, they question them. They see the church and its members as having a present contribution to make to the solution of societal problems and believe that we best advance Christ's kingdom in this world by ministering to human needs. Their text may well be: "Occupy till I come" (Luke 19:13).

The above reasoning would suggest a direct correspondence between the conservation-liberal religious spread and the conservative-liberal political continuum. But complicating factors intrude. First of all, Adventist eschatology portrays the United States republic as a persecuting power that will repudiate civil and religious liberty and enforce the "mark of the beast." Thus, orthodox Adventists find themselves in the dilemma of wanting to preserve the present governmental system and its values (as good conservatives) but of being suspicious of government trying to impose its control over the church.

Thus, orthodox Adventists are likely to oppose any public issues which may seem to break down the wall between church and state. They tend to oppose prayer and Bible reading in public schools (although they believe strongly in both where not mandated), to oppose morality legislation (though they might personally agree with the values), to oppose conservative Supreme Court justices (since liberal ones–like William J. Brennan–have been the champions of individual liberties), and to keep churches out of the political arena. In much of this they line up with political liberals. Thus, their view of eschatology influences the more orthodox to be conservative in politics generally, but liberal when religious liberty issues are at stake.

Where this factor is especially strong, the highly orthodox may take the second course noted above. Instead of supporting conservative courses and candidates, they may withdraw from the public arena altogether and proclaim: "This world is not my home; I'm just a-passin' through." Thus, a fifth of our sample claimed that they had no interest in politics; nearly a third did not identify with either political party; about a fourth stated that they had no political orientation; and two-fifths did not vote in the most recent presidential election. These "withdrawers" were most likely to be the strongly orthodox.

A second complicating factor to the conservative-liberal construct is the fact that Adventism has historically been a sort of "peace" church. From the days of the American Civil War onward, the church has recommended that its members participate in the military only in noncombatant service. This is based, of course, in the Ten Commandment law of "Thou shalt not kill" and in the Adventist belief that God has given them a special commission to carry the last message to all peoples of the world. War and killing are incompatible with the spreading of the Gospel. But, as we have seen, this stance also grows out of the Adventist view of prophecy with its suspicion of the lamblike beast. Thus, more orthodox Adventists are likely to join once again with the liberals in favoring peace actions and opposing military offensives.

A third complicating factor, as noted above, is ethnicity. Ethnic minorities, especially Blacks and Hispanics, tend to be conservative theologically and, therefore, quite orthodox. But they tend to be more liberal politically, especially in issues involving social justice. This is easy to understand in view of the history of material and social deprivations suffered by minorities in America. Though conservative in religious beliefs, these Adventists tend to stress freedom and justice over order.

To summarize, more orthodox Adventists are more likely to be conservative politically except when factors of religious liberty, pacifism, and ethnic experience lead them to believe that liberal political positions are more in harmony with their faith or personal interests. Indeed, a recurring theme in this entire study is that the Adventist involvement in the political arena is selective and that such selectivity is based on what seems to be the church's best interests. Individual members or subgroups within the church also make their decisions based on the same operating principles. Thus, it might be said that Adventists are as inconsistent as most Americans when it comes to letting pure ideology determine their political positions. However, the human mind has a tendency to organize in a way to make sense out of conflicting ideas and to reduce dissonance, and pragmatism itself is the basis for a kind of consistency.

Other Religious Measures and Political Stance

Heavy church involvement is closely related to ideological commitment. In chapter 6, we argued that the former is most likely prior to the latter. That is, as one spends more time in church activities and makes a heavier investment of money and energy in the program of the church, increased exposure to the doctrines and the need to establish consistency between actions and beliefs leads to stronger commitments to orthodox views.

Therefore, it is not surprising to find that church involvement follows a similar pattern to orthodoxy. Those most active in church-related behaviors are also likely to hold conservative political positions except on religious liberty issues.

The picture for devotional behaviors is not as clear. Those who engage in devotional practices more frequently are likely to be conservative on some issues and liberal on others. Since they are well-grounded in Adventist doctrine through frequent reading of religious literature, it is reasonable that they tend to resemble the orthodox on such issues as favoring tougher laws on crime and the basic rightness of the capitalistic system. But since time with the Lord has softened their hearts and given them a love for God's other children, they favor liberal issues like aiding minorities in need and removing racial restrictions.

Those who are more prone to subjective religious experience tend to resemble those with more frequent devotional practices. Experientials are those who sense the presence of the divine and believe that they have undergone the life-changing miracle of conversion. Since a rich devotional life fosters such religious experience the connection is clear. Those whose religion is more subjective are more likely to have social concern–aid for minorities, nursing-home insurance for the elderly, and the removal of racial restrictions–although they still retain some conservative positions such as support of capitalism. This relationship may be partly explained by the mediating effect of ethnicity. Racial minorities such as Blacks and Hispanics tend to be higher on subjective experience than Whites and also more likely to favor social-justice causes for reasons discussed above.

The intrinsic orientation to religion is a bit harder to classify in relationship to this study. Perhaps this reflects the current challenges as to what this orientation actually measures.[4] Allport felt that intrinsic religion was that which was a master motive in life and led to a love for fellow humans. Adventists high on the Intrinsic Scale were more likely to favor the elimination of racial restrictions and to support aid for minorities as the theory would predict.

On the other hand, high intrinsics revealed some conservative traits such as support for capitalism and opposition to churches becoming active in social concern. This may reflect the charge that the intrinsic orientation really measures the strength of commitment to one's religion, whatever it is, and thus is actually a proxy for orthodoxy and church involvement.[5] This would explain why intrinsics favor some conservative positions. It also explains why those high on extrinsic orientation are likely to hold liberal views. Extrinsics, in this study, are opposite of intrinsics and thus represent those who are not as committed to the teachings of the church.

The Maturity Scale is very complicated–like maturity itself. Basically, it represents (at least in part) a more open and flexible approach to religion. Thus, those who are more religiously mature (by this definition) tend to take more liberal political positions. But the picture is by no means clear-cut. The ambiguity of the relationships is probably related to the deliberate ambiguity of the scale which measured the concept.

Those high on the Grace factor–that is, they picture God in "softer" images–and those who lean toward a communitarian world view are more likely to be liberal politically for they are more likely to see the world's problems in corporate rather than in individual terms, and they are more likely to reflect the compassion of God than His sternness. On the other hand, those whose religion is most important to them are likely to split on conservative-liberal issues, suggesting that the *content* of one's religion is a more determining factor on public views than the strength with which it is held.

In chapter 3, we listed twelve hypotheses which seemed to be justified on the basis of the theoretical frameworks and historical materials that we explored. We can now see that the data from American Adventists largely support these hypotheses although the correspondence is not perfect in several cases. We have been able, however, to take this mass of diversified information and fit it into a reasonably consistent pattern.

In spite of this overall consistency, some elements seem surprising–they do not harmonize well with the overall theory and specific expectations. Perhaps this reflects, to some extent, some inadequacy in the measuring instruments. It may also signal the failure of the church to explicate clearly the consequences of its teachings for "secular" life. Or perhaps it only reaffirms the complexity of human beings and the fact that the way one mind achieves consistency may seem loose or disorganized to another mind. In the study of human behavior we are never able to remove all "error" variance. Humanity seems to be consistently inconsistent.

Chapter 11

Adventism and the Modern World

Adventism has experienced significant changes since its beginnings in the nineteenth century. The processes of social transformation in recent American society have also had their impact upon the Adventist experience. The inner transformation that Adventism has experienced is in large part due to its high educational status, urbanization, and exposure to the public sphere. Adventists have entered mainstream America, exposed to the full forces of modernity. The sect has become a denomination for all practical purposes.

Within the context of modern society, strong pressure exists to reduce the level of cognitive tension that a religious minority group experiences. As the findings show, Adventists have negotiated some level of compromise with modern culture. Perhaps the most significant accommodation to the pressures of functional rationality has been the "demythologizing" of Adventist orthodoxy, particularly among "new class" Adventists. The "new class" has responded to the forces of cultural pluralism by reducing the exclusivistic claims of their faith and by developing an ethic of civility which minimizes proselyting activities. To the pressures of structural pluralism many Adventists have tended to privatize their religion.

The symbolic boundaries which define Adventism both theologically and culturally seem to be eroding among the young, upwardly mobile Adventists. While older and minority members express clear and undeniable fidelity to orthodox statements, younger, well-educated, non-ethnic Adventists are beginning to question them. This is being accompanied by the erosion of religious commitment in its other multiple expressions. What this means to the future of Adventism is not yet clear, but it seems likely that the church of the twenty-first century will be somewhat different than the one we have known. It also seems likely that these changes will bring about new relationships to the public arena–a process that we have noted is already beginning.

Religious Civility in the Modern World

Cultural pluralism presents advantages to sectarian groups because it recognizes their legitimacy and right to compete in the marketplace of ideas. At the same time, it places great pressure on their adherents to be accepting and tolerant of people holding other religious beliefs. Thus, Adventists who have experienced greater exposure to the forces of modernity are more likely to adopt a social posture that pleads "no offense."[6] Moreover, for some, the pressure towards civility has meant little if any activity in sharing their unique beliefs, with the result of weakening their commitments to an exclusive faith. Civility, as a mode of thinking and discourse, breaks down the walls of separation that divide religious traditions, contributing to a social demeanor of accepting other faiths as equally legitimate and as also in possession of "their slice" of truth.

On the other hand, Adventists who are able to resist secularizing forces primarily through their communal attachments, as exemplified by the experience of minorities, are less likely to be affected by the ethic of civility. Strong religious communal attachments solidify and legitimize individuals' convictions about sectarian beliefs, providing the motivational structure for active involvement in proselyting activities. The presence of a close-knit community of fellow believers creates a structure that allows a particular religious world view to remain plausible even though it is disconfirmed by the larger society.[7] Obviously, all of this will have an impact on the political and social positions of individual Adventists.

These trends have already begun to have a negative impact on church growth, particularly in western societies where modernity with its secularizing forces is more visible. The very things that provide Adventists with legitimacy and acceptance within their societies (primarily education and professional status) are the factors which expose believers to modern forces which weaken religious commitments. The greater the social mobility of Adventists, the more likely they will adopt an ethic of civility, potentially limiting their church growth and, most importantly, the veracity of their beliefs. While commitments to the institutional church may remain, the character of the religious experience, particularly its historic beliefs and the life-style boundaries which define what it means to be an Adventist, are likely to be somewhat altered. Again, this may change the attitudes of members toward political and social issues and their political behaviors in ways of which we cannot be completely certain at the present time, but which will probably lead in a liberal direction.

The complexity of the cultural dynamics occurring in contemporary Adventism is that both sectarian protest and accommodationist tendencies exist simultaneously. The sectarian identity of the movement fuels its missionary drive and sustains its identity. The accommodationist tendencies enable Adventists to maintain viable educational and health institutions and gain credibility in the community of faiths.

This implies that tendencies toward accommodation are not necessarily detrimental. For example, one may be willing to adopt an ethic of civility without compromising the unique basis of one's own religious beliefs. Toleration and the granting to others a "piece of the truth" does not require any lessening of one's own commitments. It may, in fact, represent a more mature expression of religiosity. The need for civil behavior and the acceptance of the legitimacy of pluralistic world views are not necessarily incompatible with affirming a sense of priority for one's own religious group. However, accommodationist tendencies risk the potential costs of bargaining away the certainty and uniqueness of one's own religious beliefs. As mentioned, one important deterrent to this trend is the degree to which religion is experienced communally.

Communal Religious Ties

As the experience of Adventist racial minorities shows, higher communal attachments contribute to counteracting the secularizing forces of contemporary society. The cultural dispositions of Asians, Blacks, and Hispanics to familial and group attachments extend to the religious sphere, creating "communities of memory" which preserve religious commitment. This suggests that the manner in which religion is expressed–communally or individually–determines the direction of influence that

Chapter 11

socioeconomic status has on religious commitment, and thus on politics.

The experience of Adventist minorities might furnish the church at large with a mode of believing and behaving within contemporary society that has proved relatively successful at restraining the forces of modernity. However, given the fact that Adventist congregations in the United States are for the most part segregated by ethnic background, few opportunities may exist for cultural and religious exchanges.

The evidence of racial, generational, and social status differences which markedly divide the religious expressions of contemporary Adventism suggests that the future religious character (and thus the public stance) of the church might increasingly be determined by ascriptive and background characteristics as opposed to theological norms. This trend may pose a threat to the unity of the church in America.

The fact that many non-minority Adventists in this study were indifferent toward concerns for social justice is a harbinger of schism. Such schism within sectarian movements is most likely to occur when sectors within the movement are at odds with other sectors, especially over the goals that each group perceives to be implicit in the community's belief system. In short, there is evidence of social as well as theological factors which might potentially threaten the unity and integrity of the Adventist movement in the United States.

An interesting insight from this study is the dynamic interplay of different religious and social trends that exist simultaneously in contemporary Adventism, specifically concerning the church-sect typology. Minorities tend to exhibit greater sectarian characteristics with regards to their religious commitment and yet display church-like characteristics with regards to their political and social attitudes and behavior. On the other hand, many non-minorities, particularly members of the "new class," exhibit more church-like characteristics in their religious commitment and sect-like characteristics concerning their sociopolitical attitudes and behavior. Such interplay of dynamic forces makes it difficult to generalize religious-political relationships.

Privatization of a Religious World View

Structural pluralism, the segmentation of social experience into public and private spheres, has had a decisive effect on Adventism. Historically, Adventism has encouraged withdrawal from the public arena to focus on "spiritual" matters. The majority of Adventists, with the exception of ethnic groups, has also adopted an individualistic political ideology which favors the status quo.

It is interesting that despite a strong stance on the separation of church and state, Adventist orthodoxy finds close affinity with the American economic system of capitalism. Thus, while rhetorically Adventists advocate separation, in reality they are closely aligned with conservative Republicanism. This is particularly true for those with higher income levels–those who have invested heavily in the system. The question for contemporary Adventists is not whether or not to be political but how to express political sentiments in the light of their religious commitments.

Chapter 11

Evidence supporting privatization has been seen in the lack of religious impact on attitudes about collective social issues. It can be concluded that Adventist religious commitment is only a minor factor in influencing attitudes and behaviors in the sociopolitical arena. Religious symbols and meanings have failed to move beyond the subjectivity of the individual conscience into the social sphere. Moreover, it seems that economic self-interest plays a more significant role in guiding public attitudes and behaviors than do religious moral principles. To continue to fail at integrating Adventist religious teachings with the contemporary world is to fall captive to the forces of modern society.

What is perhaps the most detrimental obstruction to the Adventist mission of being the "light of the world" and the "salt of the earth" is the degree to which most members have (deliberately or unwittingly) failed to realize the social relevance of religious commitment. In an attempt to maintain singleness of vision and purity of the faith, they have in effect accommodated to the constraining forces which subjectivize and privatize religious consciousness–forces which eventually undermines the very commitments and beliefs which were being so jealously protected.

However, the study has shown that it need not be that way. Some highly committed Adventists reveal a strong degree of social involvement and political awareness. The nature of the relationship between religion and politics is–in the final analysis–elusive. Strong conservative religious commitment can find affinity with liberal sociopolitical attitudes and actions. Adventist ethnic minorities in this sample present a good example of this combination. But this position will require an intentional stance–a logical and consistent reasoning from theology to public action.

Hopefully, this research will pioneer the way for a better understanding of how Seventh-day Adventists live in this world. Perhaps the church needs to study more carefully as to whether or not the kinds of issues investigated in this study are related to the life of faith and, therefore, call for providing guidance to its members as they seek to live out their religion within their social and political communities. We believe that Christian faith has a public dimension which calls us as believers to enter cautiously and thoughtfully–but decisively–into the public arena. To this understanding of the Christian faith we now turn in the final two chapters.

References

[1] See Kenneth D. Wald, Samuel Hill, and James Guth, "Churches as Political Communities," *American Political Science Review* 82 (1988): 531-548.

[2] Kenneth D. Wald, *Religion and Politics in the United States*, 2nd Edition (New York: St. Martins Press, 1987).

[3] Ibid.

[4] For a summary of the current discussions, see Lee A. Kirkpatrick and Ralph W. Hood, Jr., "Intrinsic-Extrinsic Religious Orientation: The Boon or Bane of Contemporary Psychology of Religion?" *Journal for the Scientific Study of Religion* 29 (December 1990): 442-462.

⁵See C. Daniel Batson and W. Larry Ventis, *The Religious Experience: A Social-Psychological Perspective* (New York: Oxford University Press, 1982).

⁶John Cuddihy, *No Offense: Civil Religion and Protestant Taste* (New York: Seabury Press, 1978).

⁷Peter L. Berger, *The Sacred Canopy* (Garden City, NY: Doubleday, 1969).

Chapter 12

Overcoming the Great Fallacy

To try to improve society is not worldliness but love. To wash your hands of society is not love but worldliness.
—Sir Frederick Catherwood[1]

So far in our discussion we have described the findings of our study within the context of an interpretive theoretical framework. We have explored the nature of Adventist religious commitments and their consequences towards social and political issues. We have intentionally

Chapter 12

remained as objective and detached as we were able. However, any discussion on the nature of religious commitment and its impact on secular life is incomplete without providing some direction as to how things "should be." In these final two chapters we move beyond the question of "what is" to that of "what ought to be." We step out of our social scientist roles and don the "hats" of theologians and advocates.

We fully recognize that any discussion on this sensitive subject might elicit some degree of controversy among our readers. In fact, it is precisely our purpose to generate discourse in the living rooms and classrooms of Adventists across America. For we are convinced that greater dialogue needs to take place within our community of faith with regards to one of the most important questions–reminiscent of the rich young ruler's query–"What good thing must I do" (Matthew 19:16)? What difference do our moral commitments and values have, not just on our personal spirituality, but on the society in which we live? Does religion have anything to do with politics? Can one's private faith in God be the source and inspiration for changing social structures? Are spiritual matters, such as worship, and "secular" matters, like politics, meant to be kept separate?

And what about the church as a corporate body? Is its responsibility limited to saving individuals (i.e., plucking them out of the world and incorporating them into the body of Christ) or to influencing society by the behavior of its individual members? Or does the mission of the church include informing the norms, values, and beliefs of society? Does the church have something significant to say in shaping societal behaviors? Should it speak to issues like world peace, nuclear weapons, race relations, poverty, sexism, health care, alcoholism, treatment of criminals, etc.? How do the Biblical metaphors of leaven, salt, and light apply in the contemporary world?

These are the questions that these chapters seek to answer. Of course, we recognize that these concerns have broad ramifications requiring careful analysis. No simple answers are at hand. But while not wanting to minimize the complexity of the issues, we want to provide a theological and sociological sketch on what the relationship between religion and politics "ought to be" as we understand it.

Defining the Great Fallacy

In chapter 10 we concluded that the religious experience of Seventh-day Adventists has little discernable impact on secular political attitudes. Adventism, like other contemporary evangelical faiths, has fallen prey to the privatization influences of the culture at large, finding little to say to wider social commitments.[2] Our morality has become almost exclusively personal and private instead of also being social and public.

Christians have taken basically two approaches towards social problems. The first, the evangelistic perspective, maintains that the main task of Christians is that of winning souls to Christ. All church-related activities and programs are geared towards this goal. Most social problems, according to this view, can be solved by transforming people's hearts. Social concern is seen mainly as a wedge to reach the heart of a person. In fact, among Christians with a heightened sense of

Chapter 12

Christ's coming, like Adventists, social problems are seen as being a part of the progressive degeneration and deterioration of society that precedes the end of the world. This logic leads to an acceptance of things as they are because these predicted events announce that Jesus is at the door.

The second view, the socially involved, criticizes the evangelistic wing of Christianity as being irresponsible and unfaithful to the radical demands of justice and equality for which the scriptures call. (We use the term radical or radicalism in this book not in the secular sense, as in leftist radical, but in the religious sense of getting at the root of things, including our spiritual and Biblical roots. A radical approach then is one that tries to dig beneath the surface and get back to origins. Radical Christians are those who adhere to a life style prescribed by Scripture even when such a life style runs counter to normal social conventions.[3])

The socially involved Christians see themselves as being stewards of the earth called to hold back the winds of destruction. Evil is seen as being entrenched within institutions and structures of society. Thus, morality can be established only through active involvement in changing the structures which create the misfortune and oppression of the poor of the world. The church's responsibility should not be merely to alleviate the sufferings of the poor but to transform those institutions which mass produce poverty.

In reality both views have Scriptural basis and support in the Christian tradition. Either position when taken to extremes falls into the "great fallacy" that it is possible to separate spiritual and material concerns.[4] The evangelistic mode springs out of a Greco platonic dualistic understanding of reality, where the soul has primordial value over the body; the heavenly over the earthly. The social-concern mode emphasizes the other side of the dualism—matter over spirit, society over the individual, history over eternity. The basic theme elaborated in these last chapters is that there is a more excellent way which seeks to maintain both views in creative tension. In fact, we perceive the basic mission of Adventism to be a prophetic remnant called to maintain a holistic understanding of reality and of the message of salvation. To fall prey to either extreme of the "great fallacy" is to go against the will of God and to destroy the integrative, transforming, and salvific nature of the gospel.

We intentionally seek to elaborate more the social-concern dimension in the following pages simply because of the evidence brought out in our study that it is the more-neglected viewpoint. Thus, to some readers it might seem that we are falling prey to our own criticism of the "great fallacy." In reality, we are arguing for an integrative model which maintains in creative tension all dimensions of human life.

Adventism's Syncretism with America

Adventists, like evangelicals, have experienced what sociologist David Moberg has called "the great reversal."[5] Early evangelicalism and early Adventism, as has been shown in an previous chapter, were at the forefront of social concern.[6] However, as a religious institution grows and becomes "successful," and as it interacts more closely with its social environment, it tends to dilute the harsh

Chapter 12

and radical claims of the gospel choosing instead to domesticate and spiritualize its message. We might be surprised to discover, as findings from this study suggest, that many Adventists have been squeezed into the mold of the world around them (Romans 12:2, Phillips).

The apocalyptic metaphor of the Laodicean church (Revelation 3:14-22) captures the current status of Adventism. The description of lukewarmness is a picture not only of spiritual apathy and indifference but also of cultural and political accommodation. The Laodicean message presents a radical critique of the tendency to gain social acceptability and financial mobility at the expense of neglecting the demanding claims of the Gospel. As a community of faith that embraces apocalyptic imagery to interpret both itself and the future course of history, it is important for Adventism to understand that a major function of apocalyptic language is to arouse the moral and social consciousness of believers immersed in the murky waters of moral ambivalence and social-political apathy.[7]

The Laodicean message is a call of arousal from the state of accommodation with the powers that be, particularly those that are oppressors of the poor and weak, to radical social involvement and change. As Branson has recently stated:

> Far from providing an escape from moral engagement, John's Apocalypse is a call to arms; not to physical warfare, but to a fundamental revolt, nevertheless. Those immersed in the Apocalypse are drawn into a condemnation of the evil empire, its oppression, its ostentatious wealth, its blasphemous pretension to ultimate

authority. The taunts and threats of the Apocalypse carry out surprise attacks, execute frontal assault. Its metaphors strip Rome of its glamor, attraction, and legitimacy, enlisting the reader in a revolution of the imagination against the oppressor.[8]

Adventism finds close identification with America's mainstream values.[9]

We have perhaps created a "culture Christianity," the identification of Christian values with a particular expression of a culture.[10] In the process Adventism has lost its prophetic role in society or what Tillich called "the Protestant principle" (i.e., the capacity to denounce every historic absolutization).[11]

The findings of our study empirically verify Tom Dybdahl's prophetic and insightful assessment of the church in the 70s. He commented that the church has aligned itself so closely with its surrounding culture that "in its life-style and outlook, Adventism has virtually become Americanism. We accept America's basic social, cultural, and economic values. We support the status quo, favor conservative politics, and eagerly seek our share of America's wealth and power."[12]

Contemporary Adventism has lacked the vision for involvement in changing social institutions because we assume either that it isn't our responsibility to do so or that our nation is already conforming itself to Christian values. This phenomenon is described by sociologist David Moberg in these terms:

> A major source of the rigid equation of sociopolitical conservatism with evangelicalism is

conformity with the world. We have equated Americanism with Christianity to such an extent that we are tempted to believe that people in other cultures must adopt American institutional patterns when they are converted. We are led through natural psychological processes to an unconscious belief that the essence of our American Way of Life is basically, if not entirely, Christian.[13]

Thus the church's selection of social issues has been based more upon pragmatic and institutional self-interest than upon "a principled vision of a more humane, equitable, and peaceable society. What is worse, on some issues such as racial, sexual justice, and economic responsibility the church seems to have waited for the prodding of secular institutions, including courts, before adopting positions it should have taken on principle."[14]

Reasons for Non-involvement

There are at least four reasons why most Adventists are apolitical and tend to support the status quo. One of them is the application of the traditional doctrine of separation between church and state which we have explored earlier in this book. The basic problem, in the words of Richard Neuhaus, is that

in American jurisprudence and in the habits of public behavior, we have come perilously close to assuming that the 'no-establishment' clause has priority over a threatening 'free-exercise' clause. Again and again, in the name of 'no-establishment,' we have created what I have called the naked public square, a square denuded of vibrant beliefs, denuded of the religious, Judeo-Christian, Biblical character of the very people who possess the sovereignty by which legitimate government and law operate.[15]

To be members of a society in which political institutions function to provide equitable distribution of resources, legislate what is just or unjust, and provide adequate means to sustain a relatively good quality of life requires that we engage in asking ethical and moral questions about the order of such a society. But to ask moral questions about the nature of such institutions and their purpose is to enter into creative dialogue between the private and public language of faith. Thus to ask, "How ought we to order our lives together?" is not just a political question but a profoundly religious one. As Aristotle reminds us: "Politics is simply an extension of ethics."[16] Adventists have interpreted the separation clause as justification for noninvolvement in the political process. For some, the government represents a corrupt, futile institution, a necessary evil, while the church's main task is that of proclaiming the gospel. Getting involved in secular matters only detracts from the true mission of the church. However, this position is dangerous in that it denies the basic social nature of the human person. Biblical teaching on human nature asserts the corporeality of existence–that is, that persons are not divided into distinct separate compartments, each unconnected to the whole.

The second reason logically follows the first–the response of neutrality. The approach here is to stay out of all political and social conflicts. Better to remain "neutral" than to risk getting involved in such earthly and secular matters that will jeopardize the proclamation of the gospel. Thus, at times Adventists have passively cooperated with tyrants and abusers of human rights from Europe to Latin America, all in the name of not risking our institutional position and sapping our energies for evangelism.[17] We have traditionally been pragmatists rather than a people consistent with our application of moral principles.[18] However, it is impossible not to take sides within a democratic society. A neutral position in reality supports the side of whoever wins in the struggle for power. At times the winning side might hold positions consistent with one's moral values, but most of the time the interests of wealth, power, and social privilege win. Unconsciously, the neutrality argument leads toward conformity and assimilation of unchristian values. Moreover, it assumes that the Bible has nothing to say about how the poor should be treated and the bonds of oppression removed (Isaiah 58) or that it has any social relevance beyond changing individual hearts. Thus, for example, to fail to voice concern over the present health-care situation and to not actively work towards restructuring the health-care system is to essentially give a "yes" vote to the existing system which leaves close to forty million Americans without basic health care–primarily the poor, unemployed, children of single parents, minorities, and the elderly–in a country that spends more health-care dollars per citizen than any other in the developed world.[19]

To not get involved in voting or in effecting change on issues which will move our neighborhoods and the whole of society towards greater congruence with the principles of the Gospel is essentially to cast our influence in favor of evil. The aphorism, "All that is necessary for evil to triumph is for good men (people) to do nothing," applies to those Adventists who do not vote or who think that the church does not have a role in changing society. Thus, as Moberg has stated: "Political inaction is action in a democracy," and "most of the time action against the will of God."[20]

The third reason for the current state of affairs is that Adventists have adopted the American value of individualism. Conservatism is centered on the value of individualism. Individualism is based on several important assumptions. The first is reductionism; that is, the belief that society equals the sum of its parts–its citizens. The moral character of a nation is determined by the combined total of each individual citizen's character. Reductionism rejects the radical assumption that a social system is greater than the sum of its parts. The second assumption is individual accountability–the belief that all citizens are (or ought to be) equally responsible for their own social positions. Conservatives maintain that success or failure of a person is due to his or her personal qualities rather than adequacies or inadequacies of the system. Finally, benevolent self-interest is the belief that when citizens compete to maximize their personal interests, the welfare of society as a whole is insured.[21]

These major assumptions promote the view that all democratic institutions–religious, government, the justice system–are benign, and that social problems do not spring from the system itself but rather from individuals. Individualism sees the person bearing the major responsibility for political, economic, and social problems, thus accounting for the conservative ideological commitments of individualists.[22]

For these reasons many Christians equate political conservatism with religious orthodoxy. However: "There is no logical necessity requiring the identification of a conservative Adventist theology with conservative political, social, and economic views."[23] Christians ought to critically appraise all ideological claims, whether conservative or liberal, and select those positions most compatible with Christian ethical principles even at the risk of being considered counter cultural.[24]

According to our findings, most Adventists assume that capitalism is God's way of doing business. By implication, then, socialism is not. However, the tenets of economic individualism–reductionism, individual accountability, and benevolent self-interest–are not Biblical values but are instead secular values. To equate either capitalism or socialism with Christianity is to lose sight of the ideologically transcendent function of the gospel.[25]

The effect of individualism has led the church to maintain what we might call the "individualist principle of involvement." It says that individual Adventists can, and perhaps should, get involved in diverse social/political issues. However, the church as an official body representing the worldwide community of faith does not take a public stand on social and political matters. This position does injustice to the Biblical teaching of the church. As Jan Paulsen has stated:

Activities that individuals engage in as an expression of Christian duty cannot be on a different order from those that the church sees as her mission. The situation is intolerable if individual Christians pursue social, ethical, and political matters that the church considers alien to her mission and nature. Rigid differentiation between Christian duty and the church's mission seems contrived and difficult to sustain.[26]

The individualistic position applied to a social problem such as racial discrimination would say that minorities who really want to get ahead really can do so. All it takes to pull oneself up by the bootstraps is effort, hard work, and determination. The racism problem has to do with the question of self-determination. This view naively blames racial inequities on the minority group.[27] People who argue like this have not experienced the oppressive power of public and private institutions which limit opportunities. Individual free will is an important factor in the solution, but it operates and has its beneficial effects only within institutional contexts.[28]

Finally, influenced by the previous forces, is the existence within the religious ethos of Adventism of the "great fallacy," an overemphasis on the evangelistic mode. The dualistic understanding of the human person, the separation between body and soul, is a prevalent view among many religionists of our day. However, Adventism has traditionally held a holistic view of human nature–that it is the inseparable integration of all spheres of life. In spite of this, Adventist eschatological belief in the soon coming of Christ tends to create a dualistic thinking between the value of earthly existence and the future blessed hope. Individualism tends toward a view of hope as an abstract concept related only to heavenly matters with little consequences for historical circumstances, except when these become relevant for prophetic interpretation.

Adventist eschatology informs its mission, and mission becomes defined as spreading the Gospel for the purpose of winning "souls" (note the dualistic language) for Christ. At times it seems that the Second Coming is seen "as an excuse to shun ethical responsibility."[29] The argument goes like this: "Why care about the poor, environmental pollution, nuclear proliferation, crime, or the homeless, since after all, Jesus is coming back soon? Our efforts should be spent on evangelism." The whole gospel commission becomes a very individualistic and dualistic enterprise.

Furthermore, individualism tends to promote subjectivism and self-seeking narcissism (what is spiritually important is my relationship with God). As a result Christians tend to forget their dependence upon other members of the community, the need to respect their weaker brothers and sisters, and the necessity for action to influence society at large and its various institutional structures.[30] What we have, then, is that the individualistic and dualistic expressions of the gospel deny the very essence of the Biblical holistic understanding of Christianity.

We believe that what contemporary Adventism needs is commitment to the total demands of the gospel–accepting the unconditional grace of God and being willing to follow in the Master's footsteps. This call also means a radical change in the way Adventists perceive their communal identity and mission as a people. A truly holistic Christianity, one that holds all of its rich dimensions in wholesomely balanced relationships with all the others, is the greatest need for an effective, relevant mission in contemporary society.

The Biblical Roots of Social Concern

Any relevant discussion on the relationship between religion and its role within society at large requires an examination of the Biblical roots and images that might inform such discussion. Adventist Christians uphold the centrality of scripture as authoritative for instruction and moral guidance. Seeking a more excellent way between the dual extremes of the "great fallacy," we will conduct a short survey of the social vision of the Old Testament and New Testament, a holistic perspective on sin, and an exploration on the social implications of conversion.

Something very earthy fills the structure and message of the Scriptures. The message is not about a remote God, unresponsive to human need, but rather of a God whose very disposition towards His creation is one of deep concern, leading Him to liberating actions on behalf of the most vulnerable in society. God is found in the midst of the most desperate of human experiences –suffering, pain, and death. God reveals His character through His actions. His engagement in history testifies to the fact that spiritual realities are integrated and inseparable from secular and material realities. God does not dwell in some "sacred" realm but in the midst of human suffering (Matthew 25:31-46). We find God feeling the pain of the Jewish people and siding with them against the Pharaoh. We find Him giving instructions to devote one-tenth of income to provide for the poor and orphans; moving Nathan to confront King David with his sin; using Joseph as a political figure to prevent mass starvation; empowering a desert shepherd, named Amos, to go up and speak against the powerful for their exploitation of the poor; becoming Himself human; and showing that to know Him is to follow in His footsteps in bringing hope and alleviating human suffering.

God's invitation to His followers is not to turn away from the world into some hideaway place of uninterrupted peace but to enter with Him, bringing healing and transformation, into a struggling world where suffering, despair, exploitation, and hopelessness pervades all human experience. Let us look more closely at God's actions in the experience of the Israelites.

The Social Vision of the Hebrew Scriptures

One of the major themes running through the entire Scriptures is the Exodus. God took compassion on His people and acted according to the promise of the covenant to liberate them from the bondage of slavery. This event took central stage in the collective memory of Israel and was celebrated yearly at the Passover festival. The Exodus experience provides a clear glimpse as to the character of God and His purpose for His people. It represents not only an initiative of divine grace but calls His followers to respond in love. The ten commandments are preceded with the statement: "God spoke all these words: 'I am the Lord your God, who brought you out of Egypt, out of the land of slavery'" (Exodus 20:1-2).[31] His people's response of obedience springs forth as a result of His salvific actions in liberating His people. The Exodus experience is tied directly to other moral exhortations that begin to define the social vision of His followers:

> Do not deprive the alien or the fatherless of justice, or take the cloak of the widow as a pledge. Remember that you were slaves in Egypt and the Lord your God redeemed you from there. That is why I command you to do this.
> When you are harvesting in your field and you overlook a sheaf, do not go back to get it. Leave it for the alien, the fatherless and the widow, so that the Lord your God may bless you in all the work of your hands. . . . When you harvest the grapes in your vineyard, do not go over the vines again. Leave what remains for the alien, the fatherless and the widow. Remember that you were slaves in Egypt. That is why I command you to do this. (Deuteronomy 24:17-19, 21-22)

Other laws provided for sharing one-tenth of the harvest with foreigners, orphans, and widows (Deuteronomy 14:28-29), for lending at no interest to those in need (Exodus 22:25), and for the cancellation of debts every seventh year (Deuteronomy 15:1-2, 7-11). Moreover, every fiftieth year was designated the Year of Jubilee, during which time property that had been bought was to be returned to the family of the original owner (Leviticus 25:8-28). While there is no record in the Old Testament that this actually took place, the intention of the command was clear: the prevention of poverty and exploitation and the principle of redistribution of wealth.

This same vision was shared by Ellen G. White. Elaborating on the above principle of redistribution she wrote:

> Were the principles of God's laws regarding the distribution of property carried out in the world today, how different would be the condition of the people! The observance of these principles would prevent the terrible evils that in all ages have resulted from the oppression of the poor by the rich and the hatred of the rich by the poor. While it might hinder the amassing of great wealth, it would tend to prevent the ignorance and degradation of tens of thousands whose ill-paid servitude is required for the building up of these colossal fortunes. It would aid in bringing a peaceful solution of problems that now threaten to fill the world with anarchy and bloodshed[32]

At the center of God's action in the Exodus is His concern for justice. For the Hebrews, the idea of justice went beyond the notion of impartiality.[33] It involved a sense of fairness and wholeness among families, communities, and nation. It implied an attitude which not only favors the weak but demands that the causes of inequality and injustice be redressed. The Christian social ethic is based on the fact that God is the source of justice: "Then their number decreased, and they were humbled by oppression, calamity and sorrow; . . . But he lifted the needy out of their affliction" (Ps 107:39-41). "He raises the poor from the dust and lifts the needy from the ash heap"

(1 Samuel 2:8). Justice requires that the conditions which contributed towards maintaining oppression and poverty be eliminated.

The prophet Amos denounced those who trampled on the needy and destroyed the poor in order to gain wealth (Amos 2:6-7; 8:4-6). He spoke harshly against those who reveled in luxury while the poor were crushed (Amos 4:1; 6:1-7). Likewise, Isaiah alerted the Israelites that God will bring judgment because of their exploitation of the poor (Isaiah 3:13-15). The first task of Biblical justice is the correction of oppression. God's justice then is biased towards the weakest and most vulnerable (Ps 41:1; 72:1-4; 146:6-9). "The poor are given priority only because their wretchedness requires greater attention if the equality called forth by the equal merit of all persons is to be achieved."[34]

Finally, we know the Lord by our involvement in creating social justice.

> "Does it make you a king to have more and more cedar? Did not your father have food and drink? He did what was right and just, so all went well with him. He defended the cause of the poor and needy, and so all went well. Is that not what it means to know me?" declares the Lord. (Jeremiah 22:15-16)

Knowing has more to do with acting than with talking. Accepting by faith a God who cares so much and caring as He does for the most vulnerable is to know Him. In the final judgment, as Jesus explained in Matthew 25, God-walking is more important than God-talking.[35]

Chapter 12

How different would our world be if the ethics of the Old Testament were followed more closely. As Ellen White has written:

> If men would give more heed to the teaching of God's Word, they would find a solution of these problems that perplex them. Much might be learned from the Old Testament in regard to the labor question and the relief of the poor. In God's plan for Israel every family had a home on the land, with sufficient ground for tilling. Thus were provided both the means and the incentive for a useful, industrious, and self-supporting life. And no devising of men has ever improved upon that plan. To the world's departure from it is owing, to a large degree, the poverty and wretchedness that exist today. . . . If these principles were carried out today, what a different place this world would be![36]

These radical teachings are so central to the ethics of the Old Testament that to spiritualize them away or to deny them by not responding to their demands is to dismiss the validity of any other ethical claim of the Old Testament upon the Christian. To be sabbatarian Christians but fail to provide for the basic needs of the poor and to restructure the conditions which lead to such poverty is a moral contradiction.

In the Old Testament, worship, ethics, politics, and nature are all closely related. To separate these dimensions is not only to do injustice to the Biblical teaching but to further legitimize the "great fallacy" myth. The New Testament presupposes and reinforces the Old

Testament's call to social justice and moves beyond it by incarnating its principles in the life of Jesus Christ.

The Social Vision of Jesus

Those who maintain that Jesus' message and life did not have any political and social consequences to the established order and that He did not call for any social change or involvement in society have not understood fully the evidence of the New Testament.[37] If there is anything that we know with certainty about the message and life of Jesus, it is His uncompromising commitment to the poor in providing them hope and alleviating their physical suffering. Even before Jesus was born, His mother Mary praised God not only for His concern and liberating actions towards the poor, but also because the Messiah would bring "down rulers from their thrones but has lifted up the humble" (Luke 1:52).

He proclaimed his solidarity with the oppressed in His very call to ministry when He quoted the prophet Isaiah (Isaiah 61:1-2):

> The Spirit of the Lord is on me, because he has annointed me to preach good news to the poor. He has sent me to proclaim freedom for the prisoners and recovery of sight for the blind, to release the oppressed, to proclaim the year of the Lord's favor. (Luke 4:18-19)

The "year of the Lord's favor" was a Jewish euphemism for the Year of Jubilee, an Old Testament tradition (Leviticus 25:8-54) whereby every fifty years all

Chapter 12

the rich Israelites had to surrender property they had acquired from others, and all the poor Israelites were forgiven their debts. Thus everyone started all over again. It was, in other words, a periodic effort to redistribute the wealth of Israel. Jesus identified His mission as being in line with that of the Old Testament prophetic call to social justice.[38]

Jesus in His ethical teaching and practice stands in the tradition of the prophets; one cannot understand Jesus or New Testament ethics except in the light of that continuity.

> Woe to you, teachers of the law and Pharisees, you hypocrites! You give a tenth of your spices–mint, dill and cummin. But you have neglected the more important matters of the law–justice, mercy and faithfulness. You should have practiced the latter, without neglecting the former (Matthew 23:23).

There are two important issues in this text: (1) Jesus carries on the prophetic attack on that piety which leaves out social justice (see also Matthew 12:7; 19:16-22). (2) He clearly indicates the place of the Old Testament teachings about justice; they reflect the highest level of Old Testament ethics and are essential to his new order.[39]

By Jesus connecting His ministry to that of the prophetic tradition, He implied that the goal is a total restructuring of society.[40] His listeners were getting a glimpse of a new social order based on *agape* love–the foundation of His new kingdom. The people that Jesus identified are the poor, captives, the blind, and the oppressed. But are the poor literally poor? That is, are

254

they poor "materially" or just in "spirit"? Evidence suggests that when Luke refers to the poor, the blind, and so forth, he means those that are literally poor and blind.[41] Recent scholarship on the social political impact of Jesus' ministry attests to the radical nature of Jesus' ministry as involving social change to redress the actual material conditions of the people.[42]

In Luke's account of the great sermon, Jesus begins with these words:

> Blessed are you who are poor, for yours is the kingdom of God. Blessed are you who hunger now, for you will be satisfied. Blessed are you who weep now, for you will laugh. (6:20-21)

The same sermon is also recorded in Matthew, and while some similarities exist, the differences are particularly important. In contrast with Luke, Matthew directs the blessings to those who are "poor in spirit" and to "those who hunger and thirst for righteousness" (Matthew 5:3, 6). In Luke, Jesus not only implies that the poor and hungry are experiencing their condition literally but also names a series of "woes" addressed to the rich and the comfortable:

> But woe to you who are rich, for you have already received your comfort. Woe to you that are well fed now, for you will go hungry. Woe to you who laugh now, for you will mourn and weep. (6:24-25)

Jesus was not concerned just about the poor and outcasts but also provided healing and restoration to many women (Luke 4:38-39; 7:11-17; 13:10-13). His ministry was one of inclusiveness of all people. This included the rich when He accepted their invitations and hospitality (6:29-32; 14:1-7; 19:1-10) and even performed healings which benefited the powerful (7:1-10; 8:40-56). However, never did Jesus accept the status quo in any situation. While He visited with the rich, He also called upon them to share their wealth. He responded to the ambitions of power among His disciples with lessons of servanthood. As Cassidy stated: "Jesus' position is one of concern and compassion for people from all walks of life, but he does not passively accept values or practices that run counter to his own vision regarding healthy social relationships."[43]

The Gospel accounts contain a surprisingly large amount of evidence about Jesus' commitment to the poor and His perception that "theirs is the kingdom of heaven." He challenged the poor to "go and sin no more" and disrupted the exploitation that had transformed the temple into the "house of robbers." Jesus not only railed against the Pharisees for creating a religious system that exploited the most vulnerable but also warned them that they were becoming slaves to their own religious system which prevented them from knowing the true God. Jesus identified those people who have "eyes that do not see and ears that do not hear" as being those "whose wealth may be depriving a poor person of the necessities of life, when they fail to see that their yearning for security may be causing political oppression to peasants in another country, when they fail to sense that their religion may be geared to make them feel good about themselves and the way they choose to live rather than helping them to perceive their need of God's forgiveness and love."[44]

What we see emerging out of a closer examination of Jesus' life and ministry is a radical perspective which does not leave any dimension of human life untouched by the power of the gospel. While Jesus did not identify with or condone any of the contemporary Palestinian political options or agendas, His message and actions were those which radically threatened the social structures of the political and religious establishment. In this sense, the life and message of Jesus was political.[45] As Yoder concluded, after a close examination of the Kingdom motif in the Gospels:

> Jesus was not just a moralist whose teachings had some political implications; he was not primarily a teacher of spirituality whose public ministry unfortunately was seen in a political light; he was not just a sacrificial lamb preparing for his immolation, or a God-Man whose divine status calls us to disregard his humanity. Jesus was, in his divinely mandated (i.e. promised, anointed, messianic) prophethood, priesthood, and kingship, the bearer of a new possibility of human, social, and therefore political relationships. His baptism is the inauguration and his cross is the culmination of that new regime in which his disciples are called to share.[46]

A Holistic View of Sin

One of the areas in which we see the application of a privatization ideology on Biblical interpretation is in the Christian conception of sin. Again the "great fallacy" has been at work creating the perception that there are two distinct and unrelated views of sin–an individualist and a social conception. The individualist view interprets sin as residing primarily within individual persons. The Bible repeatedly emphasizes that all have sinned (Psalm 53:2-3; Isaiah 53:6; 64:6-7; Roman 3:23; 1 John 1:8). The sin problem is at the root of all other human problems and is resolved through repentance and acceptance of forgiveness offered by God's grace through Jesus Christ. Conservative Christians usually hold that since individuals create society, the only way to transform society is by the conversion of individuals–"a new creation" (2 Corinthians 5:17). Thus focusing on individual renewal automatically transforms institutions and political structures. This view has been a major motivation behind many evangelistic thrusts.[47] However, this view minimizes the social dimension of human experience and trivializes the complexity of social problems.

In contrast, a social conception of sin sees individuals as being the products of society.[48] They are born into a social system and socialized into its ethical values, outlook on life, and behavior patterns.[49] Sin then is located and manifests itself within society and its institutions. Personal sins are seen to be eliminated by correcting collective evils.[50]

Reinhold Niebuhr made it very clear that a moral man who is fulfilling life's responsibilities faithfully, honestly, diligently, morally, and even pietistically can contribute to evil because he is enmeshed in a social system that is evil. The nature of these systems is that the locus of responsibility for both good and sinful actions is so impersonal that it is difficult to attribute them to any one person.[51]

Mott gives many examples of social sins: absence from his family by a man whose work demands travel away from home, the institution of slavery collectively sustained in ante bellum America, administrative officers easily replaced in a bureaucracy in which decisions are made anonymously and ultimately independently of individuals, racism perpetuated by white churches, discriminatory practices of "red lining" by banking institutions in poor neighborhoods, exorbitant rents for substandard housing, white businessmen who exploit minorities by high prices and high credit charges while refusing them jobs, citizens who oppose the tax increases that would provide educational innovations to help free ghetto youth from the endless cycle of poverty, and government subsidies to tobacco companies.[52] According to the Biblical evidence (Amos, chaps. 2, 5, and 8; James chaps. 2 and 5), these practices need to be considered as sins.

The "thrones, dominions, principalities, and powers" against which Christians are warned in many New Testament passages constitute a social structuring of evil that is at the very core of the social system (Ephesians 1:21; 3:11; 6:12; Colossians 1:16; 2:10; Romans 8:38; 1 Corinthians 2:8; 15:24-26). Traditionally, Biblical scholars have associated these beings with demons. However, while demonic influences certainly are active, scholarly evidence suggests that the context in which Paul uses these terms may identify them with invisible forces that determine institutional behavior and cultural relations.[53]

Paul describes these forces as moral rules, rituals, traditions, philosophical convictions, laws, and lifestyles. They can respond to economic, political, ethical, and spiritual interests which can liberate them from their oppressive function and transform them into vehicles of justice and liberation.⁵⁴ These "powers and principalities" rebelled against God's rule. They became corrupt and sought to usurp the power and position of God. The crucifixion of Christ can be seen, in part, as a decisive battle between Christ and these invisible corrupt powers. Paul explains that in his death, Christ "disarmed the powers and authorities, he made a public spectacle of them" (Colossians 2:15). For this reason the church has been exhorted not to be intimidated by them but to make known to them "the manifold wisdom of God" (Ephesians 3:10).

At times when Christians do decide to enter into the political or economic arenas, they do so from a rather naive perspective. The systems' resistance to change and their capacity to seduce or marginalize the individual are underestimated. Difficulty also lies in not understanding the spiritual dynamism of a system. The main problem is that we tend to "essentially see systems as static, humanly conceived, and humanly driven machines. In reality they have a life of their own, a living spiritual dimension that, like a human, can resist, seduce, marginalize, or isolate those whom the system perceives as a threat to them and their power. That lively spiritual dimension of the system is its principality."⁵⁵

A holistic conception of sin, of course, will have a personal as well as a social dimension. We have emphasized the social-collective view of sin only because of Adventism's tendency to overlook this dimension. Why? It is principally due to our political conservatism, individualism, and status as middle-class members of society.⁵⁶ We tend to selectively hear only those Biblical messages that soothe our consciences and neglect those that call for radical discipleship. However, to ignore either the personal or the collective dimensions of sin is to seriously distort the Biblical message. Such narrow focus also fails to understand the true nature of society's problems.

Evil manifests itself in a very complex dynamic. As Niebuhr pointed out, the morality of moral individuals actually can help to sustain an immoral society's sinful practices and institutions.[57] Yet the opposite is also possible. To deal with only the structural aspects of human problems can easily result in overlooking the sinfulness of the individual. Christians committed to a holistic understanding of the Gospel will recognize and deal with both individual sin and social evil. As Moberg has stated: "Personal and social sins are intricately interrelated in demonic, self-perpetuating, vicious circles."[58]

Paul in his letter to the Ephesians describes the spiritual battle when he states that "our struggle is not against flesh and blood, but against the rulers, against the authorities, against the powers of this dark world and against the spiritual forces of evil" (Ephesians 6:12). Therefore, in order to resist evil, we have to heed carefully the exhortation to "put on the full armor of God," to "stand firm then, with the belt of truth buckled around your waist," to have our "feet fitted with the readiness that comes from the gospel of peace," to "take up the shield of faith," "the helmet of salvation," and "the sword of the Spirit, which is the word of God," and to "pray in the Spirit on all occasions" and "be alert and always keep on praying" (Ephesians 6:13-18). The triumph over the principalities and powers requires not human ingenuity through technology or social scientific knowledge but commitment to God's truth and justice, obedience to God's Word, and sensitivity to God's Spirit.

An enlarged perspective on the nature of sin requires that we examine the role of salvation as a social event. That is, conversion has to do not only with my personal reconciliation with God but also with my reconciliation with others in community.

A Call to Conversion

Jesus' mission involved the inauguration of a new age. He called people to conversion.[59] He began His ministry with the message: "Repent, for the kingdom of heaven is near" (Matthew 4:17). A new order has been established by Jesus that is diametrically opposed to the present order. Conversion involves a "new birth," a new beginning (John 3:3-7). All spheres of life–personal, economic, social, spiritual and political–are touched by the renewing influence of the Spirit. To follow Jesus means that all the restricting ties of the past have been broken, and a new world of possibilities has been opened. The disciples left everything to follow Jesus (Matthew 4:18-22; 19:27). Jesus' call to conversion involves a new allegiance to the kingdom of God already realized and yet to come.[60]

First-century Greeks were concerned about having a correct intellectual belief. But the early Christians were more concerned with transformation. As Wallis points out:

> The first evangelists did not simply ask people what they believed about Jesus; they called upon

their listeners to forsake all and to follow him. To embrace his kingdom meant a radical change not only in outlook but in posture, not only in mind but in heart, not only in worldview but in behavior, not only in thoughts but in actions. Conversion for them was more than a changed intellectual position. It was a whole new beginning.[61]

Conversion in the Bible is a very earthly process. It is never ahistorical or abstract. People are always called in specific historical circumstances and live out their conversion in history. While the experience is deeply personal, it is never private. In fact, "any idea of conversion that is removed from the social and political realities of the day is simply not Biblical."[62]

The most radical question for those Christians moved by the Spirit to conversion is whether they will follow Jesus and live under the principles of His kingdom. The goal of Biblical conversion is to help bring the kingdom of God into the world in anticipation of the new earth to come. Conversion from idolatry is a recurring Biblical theme. The idols of those days are very similar to today's idols: wealth, power, pride of self, pride of nation, sex, race, military might. To turn to God is to turn the back on all modern idols. To be converted to God is to surrender all of life to Him. No aspect of the life remains untouched.[63] To be converted means the end of an old order and the beginning of a new one. "When anyone is united to Christ, there is a new world; the old has gone, and a new order has already begun" (2 Corinthians 5:17, NEB). Conversion is not just the reordering of the inward self but also a reordering of that self in relation to the social world. The significance of the story of Zaccheus (Luke 19:1-10) is that he was converted to Jesus and immediately made reparations to the poor. He acted to make justice toward those that he had wronged. He recognized that he had committed social sin and that part of his conversion involved reconciliation with those whom he had exploited. His conversion to Jesus Christ involved a reversal of roles from oppressor and thief to servant and giver. To turn to Jesus is to identify with Him in the world.

The message of the kingdom to the early Christians became more than just a hope of a personal Savior; it was the creation of a new humanity where people were no longer divided into Jew and Gentile, slave and free, male and female. It was a community characterized by its protection for the weak and downtrodden and where strangers were welcomed. The believers shared their resources so that none were in need (Acts 2:42-47). Conversion then involves a radical departure from the old order of life to newness of life in Christ. Faith realizes and anticipates the transformation of all things, whether personal, social, or political, through Christ.

While conversion is an act that is entirely of divine origin, its implementation requires human cooperation. We would like to suggest some dimensions of the conversion experience in which being open to the leadings of the Spirit might help prevent a merely individualistic perspective from dominating the life of faith.

Concern for the Poor

Christians will follow Christ in His identification and solidarity with the poor. Jesus did not just identify with them; He sought to liberate them from their condition of spiritual and material poverty. Biblical justice emphasizes meeting human needs; it requires a strategic concern for the poor, the weak, and the vulnerable–not because God loves the poor more, but because they are the least likely in any society to receive justice.

> Thus, the priority given the poor and oppressed is not a denial of human equality but its affirmation. . . . The justness of any society can be measured by the way it treats those whose vulnerability make them the most likely victims of unfair treatment.[64]

In solidarity with suffering humanity Christians will find God. As Ellen White has stated:

> From what has been shown me, Sabbathkeepers are growing more selfish as they increase in riches. Their love for Christ and His people is decreasing. They do not see the wants of the needy, nor feel their sufferings and sorrows. They do not realize that in neglecting the poor and the suffering they neglect Christ, and that in relieving the wants and sufferings of the poor as far as possible, they minister to Jesus.[65]

Chapter 12

Consciousness of Human Dignity and Worth

A second element is the extreme importance of recognizing the dignity of all persons. This leads to a radical sense of awareness of the personal and institutional manifestations of sin which then leads to transformative actions to alleviate the suffering. The victims in society also need to sense their worth and become aware of their circumstances in order to become empowered to effect change.

Social Analysis

Christians need to become more informed about the intricate ways in which evil becomes institutionalized and legitimized even by religious values and institutions. Social analysis is needed in order to understand how structures such as political and economic institutions perpetuate injustice through such means as symbol and myth.[66] Such an analysis must be particularly sensitive to the complex interaction between different structures–for example, the relationship of economic and political structures (how money "talks") and those between religious and political institutions (when religious symbols and ideas legitimate the state). Failure in conducting serious social analysis will lead to short-lived and superficial solutions, without addressing the real causes of human suffering.

Community Action

Commitment to Jesus Christ involves commitment to a community. The impact of group action can have far-reaching consequences. The civil rights movement, led by Martin Luther King, Jr., is a good example of collective social action based upon a religious impulse. For example, Adventists who organize to protest the proliferation of tobacco companies' involvement in the third world can have a significant impact since the church's membership lies primarily in the third world.[67]

Community action may lead a local congregation to become involved in eradicating social ills affecting the community whether it be homelessness, illiteracy, unemployment, pornography, alcoholism, discrimination, etc.... Community action can take many different forms; setting up a soup kitchen, lobbying city hall, voter registration drives, highschool dropout prevention programs, or organizing to renovate environmental conditions in the community. Holistic discipleship demands that individual and communal action be directed at bringing hope to the most vulnerable of our society.

Political Action

"The church that educates for discipleship must also educate for citizenship."[68] Christians do not have any blueprint for the economic social order, no privileged access to socio-political questions or answers. However, as has been mentioned above, authentic conversion experience takes place within history in a particular time and place, within a particular political context. And it is within this context that believers are called to act justly.

In a democratic society, it is through the political process that change can be brought about in many important areas of social concern, both nationally and internationally. At the same time, it is vital to look beyond every historical relationship, remembering that nothing in history, nothing human, can be absolutely relied upon. Why? Because at the root human nature is selfish and corrupt. Thus, as Christians face political involvement, it is important to consider carefully before acting so as to clarify intentions as well as pretensions of political platforms and personalities.[69]

Important implications reside in the recovery of a holistic concept of conversion. For as Wallis has stated:

> In every renewal movement since the time of the early church, the true nature of conversion has been freed from the narrow limitations and restrictions imposed by the world, and the wholeness of conversion recovered. The power of evangelism is restored and the gospel again becomes a message that turns things upside down.[70]

References

[1] Quoted in Arthur Simon, *Christian Faith and Public Policy* (Grand Rapids, MI: Eerdmans Publishing Company, 1987), 14.

[2] Robert N. Bellah, Richard Madsen, William M. Sullivan, Ann Swidler, and Steven M. Tipton, *Habits of the Heart* (San Francisco, CA: Harper & Row, 1985), 231.

[3] Thaddee Matura, *Gospel Radicalism*, trans. by Maggi Despot and Paul Lachance (Maryknoll, NY: Orbis Books, 1984), 10-11.

[4] Described by Robert McAfee Brown, *Spirituality and Liberation* (Philadelphia, PA: Westminster Press, 1988).

[5] David O. Moberg, *The Great Reversal* (Philadelphia, PA: J. B. Lippincott, 1977).

[6] Donald W. Dayton, *Discovering an Evangelical Heritage* (New York: Harper & Row, 1976); Norris Magnuson, *Salvation in the Slums* (Grand Rapids, MI: Baker Book House, 1977).

[7] For a more extensive argument in favor of this reading of the Apocalypse and further references to the scholarly literature upon which it is based, see Roy Branson, "The Demand for New Ethical Vision," *Bioethics Today–A New Ethical Vision*, ed. James Walters (Loma Linda, CA: Loma Linda University Press, 1988).

[8] Roy Branson, "Social Reform as a Sacrament of the Second Advent," *Spectrum* 21, no. 3 (May 1991):49-59; quotation from p. 57.

⁹Monte Sahlin, "Who Are North American Adventists?" *Spectrum* 21, no. 2 (March 1991): 17-22.

¹⁰Rene Padilla, *Mission between the Times* (Grand Rapids, MI: Eerdmans, 1985), 15.

¹¹Quoted in ibid., 16.

¹²Tom Dybdahl, "We Should Be Involved in Politics," *Spectrum* 8, no. 3 (March 1977): 33-37; quotation from p. 34.

¹³Moberg, 42.

¹⁴Gerald Winslow, "Renewing the Adventist Social Vision," *Spectrum* 16, no. 5 (February 1986): 30-33; quotation from p. 30.

¹⁵Richard Neuhaus, "America–A Religious Republic?" *Spectrum* 17, no. 1 (October 1986): 2-5; quotation from p. 3.

¹⁶Quoted in ibid., 3.

¹⁷Jack M. Patt, "Living in a Time of Trouble: German Adventists under Nazi Rule," *Spectrum* 8, no. 3 (March 1977): 2-10; Erwin Sicher, "Seventh-day Adventist Publications and the Nazi Temptation," *Spectrum* 8, no. 3 (March 1977): 11-24.

¹⁸Michael Pearson, *Millennial Dreams and Moral Dilemmas* (Cambridge, England: Cambridge University Press, 1990), 51.

¹⁹Charles J. Dougherty, *American Health Care* (New York: Oxford University Press, 1988), 3-19.

[20]Moberg, 88-89.

[21]Richard Perkins, *Looking Both Ways* (Grand Rapids, MI: Baker Book House, 1987), 111-112.

[22]Ibid., 111.

[23]Winslow, 31.

[24]Perkins, 111.

[25]Ibid., 115.

[26]Jan Paulsen, "Is Social Service Our Mission?" *Adventist Review*, 31 August 1989, 17-20; quotation from p. 20.

[27]William Ryan, *Blaming the Victim* (New York: Vintage Books, 1976).

[28]Moberg, 90.

[29]John Brunt, *Now and Not Yet* (Hagerstown, MD: Review and Herald Publishing Association, 1987), 15.

[30]David O. Moberg, *Holistic Christianity* (Elgin, IL: Brethren Press, 1985), 32.

[31]Unless otherwise noted, all Scriptural quotations in the final two chapters are taken from *The Holy Bible, New International Version*, copyright 1973, 1978 by International Bible Society.

[32]Ellen G. White, *Education* (Mt. View, CA: Pacific Press Publishing Association, 1903), 44.

³³Stephen C. Mott, *Biblical Ethics and Social Change* (New York: Oxford University Press, 1982), 59-81.

³⁴Ibid., 71.

³⁵Frederick Herzog, *God-Walk* (Maryknoll, NY: Orbis books, 1988).

³⁶Ellen G. White, *Welfare Ministry* (Washington, DC: Review and Herald Publishing Association, 1952), 196.

³⁷John H. Yoder, *The Politics of Jesus* (Grand Rapids, MI: Eerdmans, 1972); Richard J. Cassidy, *Jesus, Politics, and Society* (Maryknoll, NY: Orbis Books, 1978); idem, *Society and Politics in the Acts of the Apostles* (Maryknoll, NY: Orbis Books, 1987).

³⁸Mott, 68; Yoder, 64-77.

³⁹Mott, 77.

⁴⁰Mott, 92; Yoder, 76-77.

⁴¹Cassidy, *Jesus, Politics, and Society*, 22-23.

⁴²See Yoder 264-77 and Cassidy, Jesus, Politics, and Society, 22-23.

⁴³Cassidy, *Jesus, Politics, and Society*, 24.

⁴⁴Robert C. Linthicum, *City of God* (Grand Rapids, MI: Zondervan Publishing House, 1991), 103.

⁴⁵See Cassidy, *Jesus, Politics, and Society*.

[46]Yoder, 63.

[47]Moberg, *Holistic Christianity*, 99.

[48]See Peter Henriot, "Social Sin: The Recovery of a Christian Tradition," in *Method in Ministry: Theological Reflection and Christian Ministry* ed. James D. Whitehead and Evelyn Eaton Whitehead (New York: Seabury, 1980), 127-144.

[49]George H. Mead, *Mind, Self, and Society* (Chicago: University of Chicago Press, 1934), 152-164.

[50]Moberg, *Wholistic Christianity*, 100.

[51]Reinhold Niebuhr, *Moral Man and Immoral Society* (New York: Charles Scribner and Sons, 1932).

[52]Mott, 12.

[53]See Mott, 3-21; Linthicum, 64-79; H. Berkhof, *Christ and the Powers*, trans. from Dutch by John Howard Yoder (Scottdale, PA: Mennonite Publishing House, 1962); Richard J. Mouw, *Politics and the Biblical Drama* (Grand Rapids, MI: Eerdmans, 1976), 86; Mark O'Keefe, *What Are They Saying about Social Sin?* (Mahwah, NJ: Paulist Press, 1990). For additional helpful exegetical and theological comments, see Albert H. van den Heuvel, *Those Rebellious Powers* (London: SCM Press, 1966); James Wallis, *Agenda for Biblical People* (New York: Harper & Row, 1976); and Ronald J. Sider, *Christ and Violence* (Scottdale, PA: Herald Press, 1978).

[54]Orlando E. Costas, *Christ Outside the Gate* (Maryknoll, NY: Orbis Books, 1982), 170.

[55]Linthicum, 78.

Chapter 12

[56]Sahlin, 17-22.

[57]Niebuhr,

[58]Moberg, *Holistic Christianity*, 102. See also idem, *The Great Reversal*, 120-159.

[59]Jim Wallis, *The Call to Conversion* (San Francisco: Harper & Row, 1981).

[60]Brunt, 15.

[61]Wallis, 4.

[62]Ibid., 5.

[63]Ibid., 6.

[64]Mott, 32.

[65]White, *Welfare Ministry*, 39.

[66]For an insightful analysis on the problem of tobacco and the third world see Charles Scriven, "Why the Marlboro Man Wants Your Kids," *Christianity Today*, 8 April 1991, 33-35.

[67]Carlos Medley, "Church Seeks Response to Third world Tobacco Sales," *Adventist Review*, 11 July 1990, 29.

[68]John Colemam, "The Two Pedagogies: Discipleship and Citizenship," pp. 35-75 in Mary C. Boys, ed., *Education for Citizenship and Discipleship* (New York: the Pilgrim Press, 1989), 57.

[69]Glenn Tinder, *The Political Meaning of Christianity* (New York: Harper Collins Publishers, 1991), 151-195.

[70]Wallis, 16.

Chapter 13

New Directions for the Church

To prevent any possible misunderstanding that might result from what we have written in chapter 12, we would like to clarify our position. We are *not* advocating that the church align itself with any political ideology (e.g., capitalism, socialism, communism), political party (e.g., Democratic, Republican), or particular political candidates. The church must never allow itself to become so narrowed and restricted. Neither are we advocating that the church use the customary methods that worldlings employ to bring about change–such as violence, revolution, media manipulation, "dirty tricks," and personal attacks on character. The church must always employ means that honor God's name and are faithful to the Gospel.

We do advocate that the church speak to social issues and that it use its moral influence to educate the conscience of society. We also urge that the church serve as a theater where the watching world can see a demonstration of how the principles of the kingdom of heaven can be applied to daily living in this world.

It is not our purpose to specify exactly to which issues the church should decide to speak nor what position the church should take nor what means the church should employ, though we do offer some examples as illustrative material. These are questions the church itself must decide through prayer, study, and dialogue. On the basis of our Scriptural survey, however, we do suggest some directions that we believe hold important implications for the future identity, nature, and mission of the church.

Evangelism and Social Concern

One of the central marks of Adventist belief and communal identity is its focus on mission. In fact, Adventism has just embarked on an ambitious program of evangelization of unreached areas of the world entitled "Global Strategy." The experience of conversion leads the believer into the world for the purpose of winning others. "Every son and daughter of God is called to be a missionary."[1] However, in light of our previous discussion, we must ask how evangelization should be defined.

Particularly, what is the relationship between evangelism and social concern?

The call for a holistic conversion experience is the goal of complete evangelism. As Jim Wallis has stated: "The most controversial question at stake in the world, and even in the church, is whether we will follow Jesus and live under the banner of his kingdom."[2] Why? Because evangelism confronts each person with the decisive choice about Jesus and the kingdom, and it challenges basic presuppositions and values about life and how one ought to live it. It confronts men and woman with a new set of rules which govern the new age over against old patterns of belief and behavior. However, evangelism, as other dimensions of religious faith, has fallen victim to the myth of the "great fallacy."

Many Christians today see evangelism as having to do only with calling individuals to a personal conversion. While the parameters of this individualist emphasis may include family, work, and neighborly environments, it fails to include the prophetic annunciation of the kingdom. Evangelism that is faithful to the New Testament will never separate the salvation of the individual from visible witness to God's kingdom on earth. What has occurred within some evangelical circles, including Adventism, is that the prophetic impact of evangelism has been domesticated and spiritualized, creating the dualism that exists between evangelism and social concern.

Adventism has gone through a "Great Reversal" retreating from their earlier social-reform interests into an emphasis upon personal evangelism which engages only those social ministries that help the victims of problems. Adventists tend to see activities such as

"Dorcas work" or health screening as baits to entice people to hear the message of salvation. That makes social ministries a means to an end rather than an end in their own right.

A very popular activity in North America among young people is to go to a developing country (e.g., Mexico, Dominican Republic, Haiti, Honduras, etc.) and spend time building a church or a school. These activities provide great opportunities for service. However, they may become domesticating types of activities which fail to examine the root causes and solutions to the plight of the poor in these nations. The mission experiences become affirmations of our nationalistic faith, of how thankful we are to live in America with our freedoms and material blessings, without critically examining the reality of economic interdependence between nations. What we fail to teach the new generation and ourselves is that the Biblical demand for justice and compassion calls into question the American system of wealth and power which consumes two-thirds of the world's resources to maintain a lifestyle that we call the "blessings of the Lord."[3] Thus we tend to deal with symptoms rather than the root causes of problems, with the casualties rather than the inflicters of human misery, with rescuing people from fires rather than putting out the flames.

Adventists, with a holistic view of reality, cannot isolate one part of the person as the locus of salvation. Salvation affects the whole person. The church does not share the Greek view of the body as a prison for the soul. As Mott has stated: "The work of God does not end with conversion, i.e., with the person as soul, soul being understood as the person in relationship to God. The person as body also is included in God's saving work."[4]

Jesus' evangelistic message was that He came to "save his people from their sins" (Matthew 1:21). This surely means that He would transform the political and social consequences of their sins as well as root out the sin itself. God's saving concern goes out to the whole of creation (Romans 8:18-23) and cannot be restricted to the private self. If a person has, through the forgiveness of sins, been freed from guilt but is still subject to perpetual conditions of suffering, then that person is not fully redeemed. We "groan inwardly as we wait eagerly for our adoption as sons, the redemption of our bodies" (Romans 8:23).

The creation waits to be set free from corruption at the time when bodies of believers will be redeemed. Transformation begins in the present and anticipates its full realization in the future. Our concern, then, must be with the whole person–with the body as well as the soul. As Ellen White explained: "The union of Christlike work for the body and Christlike work for the souls is the true interpretation of the gospel."[5]

Thus, transformative actions geared towards bringing humanization and dignity to people and freeing them from oppressive and exploitative relationships is not irrelevant to the total process of salvation. In the words of Stephen Mott:

> The body is the person's link with society, and with the uses and misuses of power. When buffeted by external forces, the whole person is affected adversely. Concern for people's salvation should arise from genuine and informed love for them as whole persons and must take into

account the relationship between the person and his or her total environment.[6]

Strategies for Social Change

In terms of strategy for social change and transformation, some argue that when one is transformed inwardly this effects changes in society, thus justifying the strategy of personal evangelism. They hold that when persons who make up society are changed through conversion, social institutions and the life of society will be changed as a result of their witness. The difficulty with this position is that it sees influence flowing in only one direction and places undue emphasis on the character of the individual to the neglect of the structures of society. That is to say, it avoids the evidence of institutional evil, which we discussed above, and the complex ways in which it manifests itself within structures of society.

Also, given our Western mode of thinking, it is difficult to understand the Hebraic conception of the human person in relationship to society. The Biblical view of the person understands the individual as being inseparable from his or her community.[7] Thus, the person is truly human only as a member of a group. A stoic and individualistic conception is foreign to the Biblical witness.[8] Finally, to see personal evangelism as the only way of creating justice is to "neglect the full imperative of Biblical justice, which includes the central command to execute justice both in the structures of society and in direct service to the needy."[9]

What we see then is that evangelism and the implementation of justice are really inseparable dimensions of the Christian faith. When Jesus "saw the crowds, he had compassion on them" and sent out his disciples to proclaim and to heal (Matthew 9:36; 10:7-8). According to Scripture, these two tasks exist side by side without conflict or subordination. In fact, faithfulness to God's task in the world will bring tangible benefits to His Church. Mott discusses these benefits and risks:[10]

1. *Witness is hurt when social action is absent.* The risk that the Christian church takes is not just one of not being credible but of not being faithful. As Michael Green states: "Our life-style, our attitudes, our concern for the sick and the suffering, the underprivileged, and the hungry, either confirm or deny the message of salvation, of wholeness, which we proclaim."[11]

If Adventists fail to realize that faith has consequences beyond the private sphere of life, they may find that their faith has succumbed to the secularizing influence of society. For the church to have a major role to play in the health industry of America, inspired by a vision of personhood and well being, and not speak on the need for basic health coverage for all Americans irrespective of their ability to pay is inconsistent with the Gospel emphasis on justice for the poor and oppressed.

2. *Witness is helped when social action is present.* If the absence of justice presents a stumbling block to evangelization, its presence can create opportunities for the gospel to be heard. Jesus said that our good work would lead people to glorify God (Matthew 5:16). Social action places Christians into diverse contexts, providing the opportunity to relate with people of all walks of life. Isolation from the world has always been a temptation

to the church. Thus social involvement in the community can break down barriers that exist between Christians and non-Christians, demonstrating the gospel in action and thus legitimizing its claims.

> When a church engages in social action and social services, community leaders and agency representatives become aware of its existence. They become favorably disposed toward it, are more likely to listen when its leaders speak to public issues, will refer people with spiritual problems to its ministries, may turn to the Christian for help in times of personal need, and are more likely to open their minds to give favorable consideration to the claims of Christ in their own lives.[12]

For some people, the claims of a holistic gospel are too radical and threatening to their lifestyles and professional involvements. However, Scripture calls for allegiance to God's reign no matter what the cost. As Paul stated, "Am I now trying to win the approval of men, or of God? Or am I trying to please men? If I were still trying to please men, I would not be a servant of Christ" (Galatians 1:10).

Social involvement may cause disruption to the evangelistic plans of some church institutions, but in reality the loss is only to a narrow misconception of what evangelization is all about. Those who pit one function over the other, as in "evangelism is more important than social action," are misguided and have used scripture only selectively.

We join the call to refuse using sentences that begin with: "The primary task of the church is . . . ," regardless of whether the sentence ends with "evangelism" or "Bible teaching" or "social concern." All of these dimensions are integral aspects of the mission of the church. These statements do injustice to the integrated framework in which these dimensions are treated in the Scriptures. The Bible is concerned about the totality of creation.

> When the church neglects one part of this concern, the other part loses vitality and is endangered. Concern for inner personal commitment to God is part of the concern for the reconciliation of all creation. Political and social concern for the created world is motivated by God's grace within the individual. As servants of God, we must make both tasks our own if we would be true to either.[13]

In a world in which life is devalued by poverty, economic exploitation, sociopolitical oppression, racism, sexism, the arms race, and plain human selfishness, evangelization needs to move beyond limited religious gestures and verbal proclamation. The contemporary situation requires an evangelization that will fulfill its intention of transmitting the good news of *shalom*, declaring publicly God's salvation and affirming God's righteous and liberating reign.[14] Holistic evangelization is threatened by pragmatic considerations which tend to override moral principles and focus on numerical growth at the expense of costly discipleship.

Biblical teaching does call for numerical growth but not in place of or above concern for the development of

Christian character and maturity. The important point is that "faithfulness to the gospel should, therefore, never be sacrificed for the sake of quantity."[15] What is needed is quantity in the context of faithfulness to the gospel. Whether or not the church is faithfully following the mandates of the gospel is the overriding consideration in all assessment of growth. It might just be that growth is occurring for the wrong reason; that is, people are being converted to a domesticated, individualistic, status quo "gospel." A time comes to ask: What type of church is it that is being multiplied?

The danger is ever present of assessing the church's mission in terms of a "market model."[16] Evangelization becomes the religious disguise of a mechanism of mass production of disembodied people which sees the bottom line–how many "souls" have been won–as the basic criterion of success. Never mind asking whether evangelization has had an impact on communities of disenfranchised minorities, effected greater accessibility of the poor to health care, created practices and values within church institutions that are equitable and just, succeeded in reducing proliferation of pornographic materials in communities, attempted to educate high-risk populations on the menace of AIDS, addressed the causes of massive unemployment in inner cities, enlisted concerted efforts at improving birth mortality rates which rival those of many underdeveloped countries, and alleviated hunger from which one in eight American children suffer. As Costas has prophetically stated:

> Whether they be multinational corporations that control, destabilize, and deform the economies of entire nations; the current

syndrome of militarization and nuclear armaments that we see around us; the dehumanizing structures of orthodox communism; the destructive powers of racism and sexism; or the myth of scientific and technological omnipotence that prevails in so many modern centers of learning, unmasking the powers and proclaiming to them God's judgment and liberation in Christ is a fundamental aspect of the church's evangelizing mission.[17]

A church that is not faithful to the gospel in all its dimensions inevitably becomes an instrument of the status quo, compromising its values to the present age.

Evangelization and Racial Segregation

Adventism finds itself in an embarrassing moral situation in the area of race relations. The church still maintains segregated institutional structures on the basis of color in most of the unions in the United States and in some other places such as South Africa.[18] While much of the secular world celebrates the benefits of a multicultural society and seeks racial integration at all levels, the church continues to operate with at least partial segregation.

Now we recognize that this is a very complex problem, and easy solutions are not readily available. The existence of separate structures today cannot be laid completely at the door of racism, although it was certainly present in their beginnings. Originally, Black conferences were created because, due to racial discrimination, many

Blacks felt that they could not achieve equal treatment within the White church structures.[19] Overseas, separate administrative units usually have been a response to surrounding racial prejudice.

Once in existence, however, such structures take on a life of their own. Those who benefit from the prestige, power, and perquisites that leadership positions in such organizations bestow almost inevitably defend their continuance. Thus, many Blacks support separate conferences (and unions) because they perceive that more leadership opportunities are provided them than would otherwise be available. Likewise, the same fear of losing power and leadership positions exists among Whites who would rather maintain segregated institutions.

Another defense for segregated institutions is the "homogeneous principle." Evidence suggests that church growth can take place more readily and more effectively among people of similar backgrounds, such as color, culture, economic status, or language and that these social divisions and groupings provide the necessary contexts for the gospel to take root and grow.[20] Related to this is the fact that prejudice in the populace may make it difficult for Christians to work for those outside their own cultural and ethnic groupings. The argument that segregated conferences provide leadership opportunities and enhance church growth does not appear to be valid and threatens to further divide the church in the future. When Hispanics become the largest minority in the North American Division within the next couple of decades, will that justify the creation of separate Hispanic conferences?

We have not been talking about separate congregations. At one time minority persons (especially Blacks) were not allowed to hold membership in many White congregations–an example of blatant racism. But some years ago, the church voted to open all congregations to any person who met basic membership requirements. We suppose that in an ideal world this would have resulted in a mixture that would have made churches indistinguishable by color. In actuality, most "birds" flocked with those of similar "feathers."

No doubt, uncomfortableness with other racial groups is responsible for some of this. But a large part also results from wanting to worship in one's native tongue or having a preference for certain styles of worship. Since all are free to make a choice, the church should not attempt to forcibly integrate congregations. The best it can do is to warmly welcome to the fellowship of each local church all who might enter and to educate the membership to an appreciation of the diversity of other groups.

The question is different with conferences and unions, as these represent segregation that is institutionally created and sanctioned by the denomination. Whatever the reasons for continuing these separate structures, they put the Adventist church in a bad light before the watching world because they belie the oneness in Christ that the church professes.[21] "For he himself is our peace, who has made the two one and has destroyed the barrier, the dividing wall of hostility.... His purpose was to create in himself one new man out of the two, thus making peace" (Ephesians 2:14-15). The issue the church must wrestle with is: Which should have the highest priority in its organization: its witness to the world of unity, love, and justice or the advantages to be gained in preserving entrenched positions and in winning some who would not respond to a cultural crossover?

Adventism, on all sides of the color line, will have to confront this reality prayerfully and with a commitment to a new moral vision of what the church was meant to be. It is time for a radical, prophetic vision that will face up to the moral contradiction of our segregated institutional structures and be willing to sacrifice status, power, and leadership positions for the sake of faithfulness to an inclusive construction of the gospel. This will not be easy. The church must implore God for a vision of how to create structures and communities that are truly multicultural in nature, that seek to respect and give voice to all members of the community regardless of race, ethnic background, and gender. But to do any less is to truncate the gospel and call into question its transformative power.

Even while we were finishing this book some hopeful events took place. Black leaders and members from the Pacific Union Conference decided against having separate local conferences as most other North American union conferences do. Instead they opted for an organization that would upgrade Black leadership positions and foster Black pastoral and evangelistic work within an integrated structure.[22]

At the same time, considering the denominational structure in South Africa, the 1991 General Conference Annual Council approved a merger of the White-dominated South African Union and the predominantly Black Southern Union Mission into a new administrative unit which was completed by the end of 1991. Furthermore, all local conferences and fields were to be integrated by the end of 1992.[23] While previously the structure in the United States had been used to justify the South African arrangements, prayerful study had led to the conclusion that "North America should not be our model for what's right and wrong. The matter of unity is a moral principle."[24] If such radical change can take place in a country which has been notorious for extreme institutional racism with its consequent violence, certainly, the society of the United States provides a more conducive context from which to restructure church institutions.

Perhaps this is the beginning of a new courage for the church in confronting the evil that lies both within and without. The church is the first fruits of the kingdom called to be here and now what God intends the whole of society to be.

> In its prophetic ministry it lays open the evils that frustrate the purpose of God in society; in its evangelization it seeks to integrate men into that purpose of God the full realization of which is to take place in the Kingdom to come. Consequently, wherever the church fails as a prophet it also fails as an evangelist.[25]

Worship as a Political Act

It has been said that "the primary social structure through which the gospel works to change other structures is that of the Christian community."[26] The church is the institution which most clearly reveals the realities of the kingdom of God. Authentic Christian community is the most powerful statement of evangelization and of a transformed society. As Michael Green has put it:

> In the early church the maximum impact was made by the changed lives and quality of community among the Christians. They made the grace of God credible by a society of love and mutual care which astonished the pagans and was recognized as something entirely new. It lent persuasiveness to their claim that the New Age had dawned in Christ.[27]

The incarnation of the Jesus story into the communal life of the church takes place at worship. For "worship is the radical center from which a Christian political presence in the world radiates."[28] Worship is the central act which creates the environment, symbols, and enactment of stories which shape imaginations and lives into the image of Christ. The story that the church celebrates and enacts in worship is not like any story told in the world; thus its politics are not the politics of any national party, ideology, or economics but the politics of the kingdom of God. Thus, the church, whose members live, marry, and work outside the periphery of its boundaries, creates a new reality, primarily through its worshiping experience, which becomes, in the words of Padilla, "an embodied question-mark," confronting and challenging the values of the world.[29]

As the "embodied question-mark" community is faithful to its worship, the deliberate and structured attempt to influence how people, themselves and others, live in society, will inevitably and naturally be "political."

It will challenge the world's understanding of personhood, presenting instead the truth of what it means to be human in relationship to others.[30] The message of the kingdom becomes more than an ideal. Commenting on the life of the early church, Wallis stated:

> A new human society had sprung up, and it looked very much like the new order to which the evangelists pointed. Here love was given daily expression; reconciliation was actually occurring. People were no longer divided into Jew and Gentile, slave and free, male and female. In this community the weak were protected, the stranger welcomed. People were healed, and the poor and dispossessed were cared for and found justice. Everything was shared, joy abounded, and ordinary lives were filled with praise.[31]

Worship is the church's distinct and indispensable activity which celebrates God's work in reconstituting identities and vision. It is the fountain from which political inspiration and action flow.[32] There is no Biblical source which explores this interrelationship better than Isaiah 58.

The Marriage of Worship and Justice

Adventist have traditionally used this chapter to define themselves. Ellen White goes so far as to say that Isaiah 58 contains "the message for this time," one that "is of the highest importance."[33] She counseled those who claimed to be children of the light but "who have felt so reluctant to inconvenience yourselves by favoring the needy" to read the chapter again and again: "You whose hearts and houses are too narrow to make a home for the homeless, read it; you who can see orphans and widows oppressed by the iron hand of poverty and bowed down by hardhearted worldlings, read it."[34] Those words speak prophetically. Let us examine the chapter in more detail.[35]

The close relationship between worship and justice appears clearly in Isaiah 58. God's people have been living comfortably with the "great fallacy." Notice what happens when God speaks to them. The background of the passage (Isaiah 58:1-12) is that God is highly displeased with the introspective, privatistic, individualistic, and status quo character of the people's worship and instructs the prophet to make His displeasure clearly known without a shadow of a doubt: "Shout it aloud, do not hold back. Raise your voice like a trumpet," and confront the people with their sins (vs. 1).

The people are in total shock that they are being rebuked for, after all, they "seem eager to know my ways" and seem "eager for God to come near them" (vs. 2). Fasting had become the principal pious exercise and can stand as a symbol for any kind of worship or practice done with the objective of securing God's favor.

Thus, when God rebukes them, they react as if to say: "Haven't we been going the extra mile? Doesn't God take notice of how sincere and pious we are?" As a result they reasoned: "Why care to be religious if God is not going to take notice?"

> "Why have we fasted," they say,
> > "and you have not seen it?
> Why have we humbled ourselves,
> > and you have not noticed?" (vs. 3)

They asked a question, and God immediately answered them:

> Yet on the day of your fasting [in the midst of your religious practices], you do as you please and exploit all your workers. (vs. 3)

They are probably wondering what, if anything, does worshiping God have to do with providing minimum wages to workers or health-care insurance for the poor. God is not pleased and does not even attend to those who pretend to be enacting worship. "You cannot fast as you do today and expect your voice to be heard on high" (vs. 4).

> God's voice becomes somewhat harsh: "Is that what you call a fast, a day acceptable to the Lord" (vs. 5)?

He is ready now to show the people the real meaning and manner of conducting worship. "You want to know my idea of a real fast?" God exclaims. I will tell you:

> Is not this the kind of fasting I have chosen:
> > to loose the chains of injustice
> > and untie the cords of the yoke,
> to set the oppressed free
> > and break every yoke?

Is it not to share your food with the hungry
>and to provide the poor wanderer with shelter–
when you see the naked, to clothe him,
>and not to turn away from your own flesh and blood? (vss. 6-7)

If the message is not clear, God goes even further to explain the real meaning of worshiping:

If you do away with the yoke of oppression,
>with the pointing finger and malicious talk,
and if you spend yourselves on behalf of the hungry
>and satisfy the needs of the oppressed,
then your light will rise in the darkness,
>and your night will become like the noonday." (vss. 9-10)

Then life will be dramatically different. God promises a life full of hope and fulfillment. Notice, however, that the social agenda spelled out in these verses is not the social platform of a local political group or the community service plan of the local synagogue. Rather, it is a definition of what it means to be a worshiping community. The guiding principle of worship is the creation of justice.

To worship "radically" (in the sense of getting at the root of what God requires) is to be thrust into a "radical" political stance (in the sense of working towards how things should be, rather than a cosmetic touching up of the way things are). This overlap can be seen clearly in the successive uses of the image of the "yoke" in the passage.

A yoke was worn by a beast of burden and implied subservience to whoever was driving the beast. To put a yoke on the neck of a person, as the Isaiah passage does, is to reduce that person to the level of a beast–to make that person subhuman. How is this situation to be overcome? The prophet outlines three steps, each more "radical" than its predecessor.

1. *"Loose the chains of injustice and untie the cords of the yoke" (vs. 6).* This means to make the burden less painful and to provide some immediate relief from it; in other words, to alleviate some of the immediate conditions of social evil.

2. *"Break every yoke" (vs. 6).* This is a more demanding challenge. It calls for God's people to destroy the social structures symbolized by the yoke, whatever they are, that condemn people to live subhuman lives.

3. *"Do away with the yoke of oppression" (vs. 9).* They are not to leave even the remains around but to do away with all the structures of oppression so as never again to be tempted to dominate and subjugate people but rather to allow justice and peace to reign.

The action goes beyond simple charity to attack the causes of suffering and oppression. The will of God for His people is that they engage in those activities which will bring an end to human suffering. Ellen White understood this principle when she spoke against injustices being committed against a blind man. She alludes to the text in Isaiah when she states:

> God requires that His people should not allow the poor and afflicted to be oppressed. If they break every yoke and release the oppressed, and are unselfish and kindly considerate of the needy, then shall the blessings promised be theirs. . . . The stumbling block referred to in the word of

lives where they left off–thankful for the refreshing moments of spiritual ecstasy.

However, these experiences may be viewed from a different perspective. They can and should be seen as windows into the normative life revealing the disparity between "what is" and "what ought to be." These ecstatic encounters should function to provide daily lives with the mores, values, and manner of acting suitable to those under the Lordship of Jesus Christ. Thus, these moments of silent spirituality are meant to be descriptive of what life "ought" to be. "The Lord's Supper is not meant to be the extraordinary meal but the ordinary one, the meal that is the model for all other meals. The way bread is shared on this occasion is the way bread is meant to be shared on all other occasions."[39]

The Lord's Supper celebrations proclaim to those that cannot afford to eat to come anyway because there is no charge. Do not be afraid of joining in because no distinctions between upper and lower classes, rich and poor, male and female remain; everyone is on the same footing, and the equality is an equality of need. The above perspective helps illuminate Paul's difficult warning that believers can eat and drink at the Lord's table to their own damnation (1 Corinthians 11:27-29). It suggests that one way of eating and drinking to one's own damnation may be to accept food from the Lord's table without making sure that food is on the tables of the poor.[40]

These enactments move communities from being status quo to seeking transformative changes in their world based on the inspiration of their worship experiences. "Only where there is doxology can there be justice, for such songs transfigure fear into energy."[41]

Chapter 13

Renewing the Adventist Social Vision

We have set out to provide a Biblical and sociological rationale for the position that religious faith, if truly representing its Biblical roots, must and will have political consequences that are faithful with the agenda of the kingdom of God. We have intentionally overemphasized certain dimensions simply to advance thinking in areas that, from our perspective, the general culture of Adventism has neglected. However, we fully concur with John Stott of "the folly of unnecessary polarization" between the intellect and emotion, conservative and liberal, form and freedom, evangelism and social action. Biblically speaking, the truth does not lie in either a golden mean somewhere in the middle between them or in one of the extremes. Rather, it lies in both extremes. Hence, "we have good Biblical warrant to replace a rather naive either-or with a mature both-and. Let us place our feet confidently and simultaneously on both poles."[42]

The Adventist church, which claims the whole world as its mission field and wants to proclaim faithfully the whole gospel, must make the *kerygmatic* encounter with the structures that dominate and oppress human life an indispensable dimension in its mission agenda. The temptation to accommodate to the "spirit of the age" rather than to the spirit of Christ, to compromise Christian convictions rather than to stand firm on the Lord's calling, and to be more loyal to "market model" techniques than to the values of God's kingdom is ever before the church. Subtle and overt pressures are brought to bear upon institutions that are committed to God's liberating mission.[43]

The prophetic tradition challenges Adventism to confront head-on oppressive structures like consumerism, militarism, multinational capitalism, international communism, racism, and sexism–bringing criticism and changes based on the values of the new kingdom and hope for a renewed tomorrow. In the words of missiologist, Orlando Costas: "We need a spirituality of missional engagement: a devotional attitude, a personal ethic, a continuous liturgical experience that flows out of and expresses itself in apostolic obedience."[44] A devotional spirituality of prayer, Bible study, personal ethics, and worship does not mean withdrawal from the world but an immersion in its sufferings and struggles. Likewise participation in the struggles of history does not mean an abandonment of spirituality and worship, but an experience of God from the depths of human suffering.

> Mission without spirituality cannot survive any more than combustion without oxygen. The nature of the world in which we live and the gospel that we have been committed to communicate therein demand, however, that it be a spirituality of engagement and not of withdrawal. Such a spirituality can only be cultivated in obedience and discipleship, and not in the isolated comfort of one's inner self. By the same token, it can only be verified in the liberating struggles against the principalities and powers that hold so many millions in bondage.[45]

Chapter 13

Prophetic Voices in Adventism

Adventists need a more authentic Biblical theology–one which seeks to maintain the integrative nature in which the Bible presents the radical and consequential aspects of faith. Adventist preachers need to understand the holistic nature of the gospel and dare to speak about poverty, justice, and economics as frequently as does Scripture. Only then will contemporary Adventists live up to their identity as a "remnant" people, fully identified with the costly way of the cross.[46]

New reason for encouragement, however, is springing up all around. Recent books published by Seventh-day Adventists are beginning to address the social relevance of Adventism and call for a balanced, holistic understanding of the gospel. Already cited in this or the previous chapter are John Brunt's *Now and Not Yet*, Pedrito Maynard-Reid's *Poverty and Wealth in James*, Michael Pearson's *Millennial Dreams and Moral Dilemmas*, and Caleb Rosado's *Broken Walls*. Two additional examples are Rosado's *What Is God Like?* and Charles Scriven's *The Transformation of Culture*.[47]

Articles in Adventist journals have also been advocating social responsibility. An editor of the *Adventist Review* noted that

> there has always been a very strong social element in God's prophetic message to this covenant people. Conservative evangelical Christians, Adventist included, stand in grave danger of forgetting this.... Why can't we 'reach out and touch someone and make this world a better place if we can,' while at the same time

pointing people to the scriptural realism that 'here have we no continuing city, but we seek one to come' (Heb 13:14, KJV). To be faithful to the gospel is to learn how to do both.[48]

Has Adventism lost its prophetic edge by failing to speak relevantly to contemporary society? As Mitchell Tyner stated: "Those who hold themselves above the world, in exclusivity, are not often actively opposed; they are simply ignored." He called for a "constructive engagement with society" which will result in greater balance and relevance to the message–thus fulfilling the "lofty purpose for which Adventism came into being." To be sure:

> This does not call for the church to involve itself in political questions. It is a call for the church to speak to issues. The church, for instance, may–and must–speak on behalf of the dignity and equality of every person, but without involving itself in the political mechanics necessary to achieve that goal.[49]

An article written by the president of the Trans-European Division, Jan Paulsen, sought to answer the question of whether or not social service is part of the Adventist mission. The church's mission is that of "presenting Christ to the world" and demonstrating that acceptance of God's gift of salvation will mean a different way of life. "Salvation is not an act of withdrawal from the surrounding world. . . . Personal salvation finds inevitable expression in social concerns." Arguing against dualistic tendencies, he states that to

> narrow one's definition of mission to preaching the Word, baptizing, and establishing churches, while placing other activities for which we have a Biblical command outside the church's mission, seems unwarranted. . . . Jesus did not present a choice between satisfying physical hunger and spiritual hunger, between being healed and being eternally saved, between being lifted up from deprivation and alienation and being offered eternal life. Neither must the church in its mission be caught between false choices.[50]

Also, Adventist sociologist Charles Teel has been investigating the social history of the Adventist church in Peru and has found that early missionary pioneers, Fernando and Anna Stahl, did not simply conduct traditional missionary activities but were radically involved in changing the oppressive structures of society among the Peruvian Indians, primarily through education.[51]

Recent articles have addressed concerns related to the tobacco industry.[52] Newly elected church president Robert Folkenberg told the delegates to the 1990 World Session of Seventh-day Adventists that the time had come for the Adventist church to become more active in the anti-tobacco movement. The international nature of the church puts it in a good position to work with government agencies and other international organizations to develop coalitions that can bring change.

Jack Provonsha has proposed that the cosmic conflict demands that the Adventist church be a part of a prophetic minority that, like the prophets, is deeply disturbed by hypocrisy and injustice. "A prophetic movement, insofar as it is true to its divine calling, may function as a catalyst for bringing about that final polarization which constitutes the climax of the Great Controversy."[53]

In two other recent examples Manuel Vasquez described the increasing influence of ethnic minorities, women, singles, and the handicapped within the North American church, and Doug Morgan, in a reflection on Martin Luther King, Jr., harmonized the Advent hope with concern for social justice.[54] Earlier we mentioned things such as position papers released at the 1990 World Session and President Wilson's call to the Soviet government for world peace. Though resistance continues, more and more leaders have been convicted of the need to don the prophetic mantle and speak for social justice.

Conclusion

We believe that God has called the Adventist church to be a witnessing prophetic community of integrity and fidelity to the holistic message of salvation. It is called to proclaim and live the present and future realization of God's promised kingdom. To live up to the demands of being a "remnant" community, Adventists must consider the call to radical social involvement as being an integral part of its commitment to the lordship of Jesus Christ. Adventism needs to make a radical shift in its self-understanding and in its relationship to secular society. The scope and nature of its involvement will be determined by its collective moral conversations, toward which we hope this book will contribute.

Chapter 13

In the final analysis whether to be involved in politics or not is not really the question. The fact is, as Padilla has stated, that

> whether we like or not, we are already involved. Politics and economics are unavoidable; they are part of the reality that surrounds us while we are in the world. The real question, therefore, is: Since we are in fact involved, how can we make sure that our involvement is faithful to the gospel of our Lord Jesus Christ? The problem is that even though we may try to avoid taking any notice of politics and economics, they always take notice of us.[55]

In 1986, Gerald Winslow wrote the following statement: "A religious movement that grows beyond sectarian seclusion but fails to find a modern, prophetic vision is doomed to worldliness."[56] In light of the findings of this study, we suggest that Seventh-day Adventism is facing this prospect.

The light of the dawn will appear when, in the words of Isaiah, we become "repairers of broken walls"– repairers of the "great fallacy" which so pervades our religious consciousness. The promise of the prophet is one of renewal and awakening revival: "If you do away with the yoke of oppression. . . . You will be like a well-watered garden, like a spring whose waters never fail" (Isaiah 58:9,11).

God does not mean a block of wood placed before the feet of the blind to cause him to stumble, but it means much more than this. It means *any course that may be pursued to injure the influence of their blind brother, to work against his interest, or to hinder his prosperity* (emphasis supplied).[36]

Among the prophets, social justice was regarded as being so crucial to faith that without it any form of religious devotion and piety was worthless (Amos 5:21-24; Micah 6:6-8).[37] The point of Isaiah 58 and similar passages is not so much to condemn the worships and sacrifices but rather to point out that the "great fallacy" exists when social justice is totally absent. "Worship is defined by how we act for justice, and how we act for justice defines our worship."[38]

Worship as Enactment of a New Community

Worship is not simply a celebration of praise to God, but it involves the enactment of the life of a new community. Traditionally, worship enactment celebrations in Adventism center around the celebration of the Lord's supper, foot washing, baptism, and the Sabbath.

These worship experiences are often viewed primarily as breaks in the weekly routine of work, study, and family chores. Once a week, ordinary lives are interrupted by a worship celebration, the ecstatic experience of a musical concert, the celebration of the Lord's supper, or a baptism. For a brief period these experiences intervene in the flow and sameness of daily existence. Then afterwards, the worshipers pick up their

References

[1] Ellen G. White, *The Ministry of Healing* (Mt. View, CA: Pacific Press Publishing Association, 1942), 395.

[2] Jim Wallis, *The Call to Conversion* (San Francisco: Harper & Row, 1981), 16.

[3] See Ronald J. Sider, *Rich Christians in an Age of Hunger* (Downers Grove, IL: Inter-Varsity Press, 1980).

[4] Stephen C. Mott, *Biblical Ethics and Social Change* (New York: Oxford University Press, 1982), 118.

[5] Ellen G. White, *Welfare Ministry* Washington, DC: Review and Herald Publishing Association, 1952), 33.

[6] Mott, 119.

[7] Ibid.

[8] Ernest G. Wright, *The Biblical Doctrine of Man in Society* (London: SCM, 1954), 47.

[9] Mott, 113.

[10] Ibid., 123-126.

[11] Michael Green, *Evangelism in the Early Church* (Grand Rapids, MI: Eerdmans, 1970), 176.

[12] David O. Moberg, *The Great Reversal* (Philadelphia: J. B. Lippincott, 1977), 159.

Chapter 13

[13]Mott, 127.

[14]Orlando Costas, *Liberating News: A Theology of Contextual Evangelization* (Grand Rapids, MI: Eerdmans, 1989), 46.

[15]Rene Padilla, *Mission between the Times* (Grand Rapids, MI: Eerdmans, 1985), 33.

[16]Peter Berger, "A Market Model for the Analysis of Ecumenicity," *Social Research* 30, no. 1 (Spring 1963): 77-94.

[17]Orlando Costas, *Christ Outside the Gate* (Maryknoll, NY: Orbis Books, 1982), 171.

[18]See Eric C. Webster, "South African Churches Call Apartheid Sin," *Spectrum* 21, no. 2 (March 1991): 9-16.

[19]Joe Mesar and Tom Dybdahl, "The Utopia Affair," *Adventist Heritage*, January 1974, 34-41, 53-54.

[20]C. Peter Wagner, *Our Kind of People: The Ethical Dimensions of Church Growth in America* (Atlanta: John Knox Press, 1979).

[21]Caleb Rosado, *Broken Walls* (Boise, ID: Pacific Press Publishing Association, 1990).

[22]Earl Canson, "Pacific Union Blacks Recommend Administrative Modification," *Adventist Review*, 2 May 1991, 21-23.

[23]A. Bediako, "Miracle in South Africa," Adventist Review, 6 February 1992, 12-13.

[24] Carlos Medley, "Progress in South Africa: SA Commission Brings Encouraging Reports," *Adventist Review*, 2 May 1991, 6.

[25] Padilla, 31.

[26] John H. Yoder, *The Politics of Jesus* (Grand Rapids, MI: Eerdmans, 1972), 157.

[27] Green, 120.

[28] Robert E. Webber and Rodney Clapp, *People of the Truth* (San Francisco: Harper & Row, 1988), 5.

[29] Padilla, 169.

[30] Webber and Clapp, 12.

[31] Wallis, 15.

[32] Webber and Clapp, 68.

[33] White, *Welfare Ministry*, 29.

[34] Ibid, 28.

[35] In our discussion of Isaiah 58, we follow the insights of Robert McAfee Brown, *Spirituality and Liberation* (Philadelphia: Westminster Press, 1988), 125-130.

[36] Ellen G. White, *Testimonies for the Church*, 9 vols. (Mountain View, CA: Pacific Press Publishing Association, 1948), 3:519.

[37]For a similar conclusion from an analysis of wealth and poverty in the book of James, see Pedrito U. Maynard-Reid, *Poverty and Wealth in James* (Maryknoll, NY: Orbis Books, 1987).

[38]Brown, 130.

[39]Ibid., 94.

[40]Ibid., 92-95.

[41]Walter Brueggeman, *The Prophetic Imagination* (Philadelphia: Fortress Press, 1983), 27.

[42]John R. W. Stott, *Balanced Christianity* (Downers Grove, IL: InterVarsity Press, 1975), 43.

[43]Costas, *Christ Outside the Gate*, 171.

[44]Ibid., 172.

[45]Ibid.

[46]Charles Scriven, "The Real Truth about the Remnant," *Spectrum* 17, no. 1 (October 1986): 6-13.

[47]Caleb Rosado, *What Is God Like?* (Hagerstown, MD: Review and Herald Publishing Association, 1988); Charles Scriven, *The Transformation of Culture* (Scottdale, PA: Herald Press, 1988).

[48]Roy Adams, "To Walk Humbly," *Adventist Review*, 9 March 1989, 10-12.

⁴⁹Mitchell A. Tyner, "The Church and Society," *Adventist Review*, 4 January 1990, 14-15.

⁵⁰Jan Paulsen, "Is Social Service Our Mission?" *Adventist Review*, 31 August 1989, 17-20.

⁵¹Charles Teel, "The Radical Roots of Peruvian Adventism," *Spectrum* 21, no. 1 (December 1990): 5-18.

⁵²See Scriven, "Why the Marlboro Man Wants Your Kids," and Carlos Medley, "Church Seeks Response to Third World Tobacco Sales," *Adventist Review*, 11 July 1990, 29.

⁵³Jack Provonsha, "The Church as a Prophetic Minority," *Spectrum* 12, no. 1 (September 1981): 23.

⁵⁴Manuel Vasquez, "Emerging Voices in the Church," *Adventist Review*, 4 January 1990, 12-13; Doug Morgan, "The Millennium and Dr. King," *Adventist Review*, 22 February 1990, 18-19.

⁵⁵Padilla, 41-42.

⁵⁶Gerald Winslow, "Renewing the Adventist Social Vision," *Spectrum* 16, no. 5 (February 1986): 30-33.

Appendix

Methodology of the Study

or those readers who desire specific details as to the manner in which this research was planned and executed, this brief appendix is included.

The study was conducted by the Institute of Church Ministry (ICM) at the Seventh-day Adventist Theological Seminary, Andrews University. Basic expenses of the research were covered by a faculty research grant awarded to Drs. Roger Dudley and Sara Terian. Research salaries were covered by a sustaining grant to ICM provided by the North American Division of Seventh-day

Adventists which also granted permission and lent moral support. The Institute of Hispanic Ministry at the Seminary also provided a small grant.

The research instrument was developed first by choosing or constructing various scales to measure dimensions of religiosity that a thorough review of the literature suggested might be relevant. These scales have been explained in detail in the text. A list of public issues was chosen and incorporated along with questions on political party, voting preference, and political orientation. Finally, the appropriate demographic variables were added.

The first draft of the questionnaire was submitted to specialists in sociology, Adventist studies, public affairs, and measurement as well as to church leaders. Their suggestions were incorporated in the revisions. The final draft consisted of eighty-two questions in a variety of response choices. A copy is included at the end of this appendix. In final form, eighteen statements on public issues were explored. The potential list was more than twice this long but was reduced to the present size by attempting to select a battery of items that would be representative (rather than exhaustive) of the most-debated public concerns of the day.

The sample was created by drawing 800 households by a random sequential method (every Nth name after a random starting point) from the mailing list of the North American Division edition of the *Adventist Review*, the general church paper of Seventh-day Adventists. While this journal is published weekly and sold by yearly subscription, church administration subsidizes the sending of the first issue of every month on a complimentary basis to every Adventist household in the

Appendix

United States and Canada as far as the list is complete. Since maintaining a current list is a major undertaking, this process is likely to under represent those members who have recently changed addresses, especially inactive members who do not bother to report the changes as well as minorities, particularly non-English-speaking groups. Some 300,000 names are on the monthly list. While the list is not perfect, it is certainly the best Adventist national list in existence. Permission for the drawing was secured from the administrative officers of the Division, and the actual selection of names was performed by the Research and Development Office of the Review and Herald Publishing Association, the custodian of the list.

It must be emphasized that the data tend to under represent the ethnic minority groups in the North America Division. This was not the intention of the researchers. However, it resulted from the inherent biases and limitations of the national list and economic limitations. A more effective way of increasing ethnic representation would have been to over sample the major ethnic groups–African-Americans, Latinos, and Asian-Americans. This would have included translating the instrument into at least the Spanish language. However, the research funds available limited the opportunity of using extensive procedures to increase minority representation. This is an unfortunate limitation of this research, particularly since comparative analysis between nonwhite and white groups elicited some important differences.

To assess the impact of minority attitudes on religious and political attitudes we collapsed the African-American, Latino, and Asian groups into a new variable called "minorities." Theoretically, there is a problem with this procedure given that these are different groups with quite different experiences both religiously and socially. Nevertheless, the analysis elicited significant differences that enabled us to begin to theorize, although tentatively, about some general trends.

We both recognize that many research endeavors among Adventists in the United States have excluded minority representation. In fact, we can no longer assume that a random selection process of a sample will elicit a truly representative sample because of the multiethnic nature of society. For example, random samples are usually biased against Hispanics–failing to include adequate representation from the different Hispanic subgroups such as Cubans, Mexican-Americans, and Puerto Ricans. One would have to sample proportionately across Hispanic subgroups according to their geographic location–Puerto Ricans in the East Coast, Cubans in South Florida, Mexican-Americans in the West and Southwest.

Thus while recognizing the limitations of the research, with respect to ethnic minority representation, we have found some interesting differences with important theoretical consequences which we have taken the liberty to expound. We are committed to future research endeavors that will seek to be truly representative and urge other researchers to do the same.

These data may have other limitations as well. For example, it is possible–even likely–that some respondents were not well enough informed on some of the issues to take a position that reflected their basic political and/or religious orientation. This situation could account for some of the apparent inconsistency. Other subjects might not have been completely truthful, tending to give answers that they considered more socially desirable.

All surveys suffer to some extent from these limitations. Yet the range of answers was still great enough to provide for significant correlations. While this research does not reveal all the truth, it nevertheless reveals more truth than we have had up until now. With whatever limitations it possesses, we believe that this study makes a valuable contribution to a neglected area.

The North American Division includes both Canada and Bermuda. However, since public issues are somewhat different in these countries, Canadian and Bermudian addresses were eliminated from the sample and only households in the United States were selected.

Since several members may comprise a household, the instructions accompanying the questionnaire contained a further sample selection procedure. Recipients were told that the survey must be completed by a baptized member of the Adventist church who was at least 18 years old. In case more than one member of the household met these criteria, the one whose birthday came first in the calendar year was to complete the questionnaire.

The data were collected in 1988. Copies of the questionnaire, letters of appeal and instruction, and a stamped envelope addressed back to ICM were mailed to the 800 households. Two additional mailings followed several weeks apart. Each included another questionnaire and another stamped envelope. In addition, we telephoned the Hispanic names on the list in an effort to increase response from that subsample. In spite of this extra effort, Hispanics comprise only about 3% of the sample while they make up about 8% of the membership

Appendix

of the Division. This under representation may be partially due to the fact that the questionnaire was available only in English. Thus these findings may not fairly represent the attitudes of all Hispanic Adventists in North America.

It was found that 52 of the letters were undeliverable due to incorrect addresses, thus reducing the sampling frame to 748. Of these 419 completed usable instruments, resulting in a response rate of 56%. The analyses presented in the book are based on these 419 subjects.

RELIGION AND PUBLIC ISSUES SURVEY

Please indicate the extent of your agreement with the following statements by circling the appropriate number as indicated: 1=strongly disagree 2=somewhat disagree 3=uncertain 4=somewhat agree 5=strongly agree

		strongly disagree				strongly agree
1. God created the world in six literal days, approximately 6000 years ago.		1	2	3	4	5
2. A person's standing before God is based on his/her obedience to God's law.		1	2	3	4	5
3. The investigative judgment began in the second apartment of the heavenly sanctuary on October 22, 1844.		1	2	3	4	5
4. Jesus Christ will come the second time in our generation.		1	2	3	4	5
5. The Seventh-day Adventist Church is God's true church.		1	2	3	4	5
6. Ellen White was inspired by God, and her writings are an authoritative guide for Adventists today.		1	2	3	4	5
7. I frequently feel very close to God in prayer, during public worship, or at important moments in my daily life.		1	2	3	4	5
8. I often experience the joy and peace which comes from knowing my sins have been forgiven.		1	2	3	4	5
9. I am certain that I have had a conversion or born-again experience.		1	2	3	4	5
10. My faith involves all of my life.		1	2	3	4	5
11. One should seek God's guidance when making every important decision.		1	2	3	4	5
12. In my life I experience the presence of the Divine.		1	2	3	4	5
13. My faith sometimes restricts my action.		1	2	3	4	5
14. Nothing is as important to me as serving God as best I know how.		1	2	3	4	5
15. I try hard to carry my religion over into all my other dealings in life.		1	2	3	4	5
16. My religious beliefs are what really lie behind my whole approach to life.		1	2	3	4	5
17. It doesn't matter so much what I believe as long as I lead a moral life.		1	2	3	4	5
18. Although I am a religious person, I refuse to let religious considerations influence my everyday affairs.		1	2	3	4	5
19. Although I believe in my religion, I feel there are many more important things in life.		1	2	3	4	5
20. My religious beliefs provide me with satisfying answers at this stage of my development, but I am prepared to alter them as new information becomes available.		1	2	3	4	5
21. I am happy with my present religion but wish to be open to new insights and ways of understanding the meaning of life.		1	2	3	4	5
22. As best as I can determine, my religion is true, but I recognize that I could be mistaken on some points.		1	2	3	4	5
23. Important questions about the meaning of life do not have simple or easy answers; therefore faith is a developmental process.		1	2	3	4	5

Institute of Church Ministry   1988

	strongly disagree				strongly agree
24. I could not commit myself to a religion unless I was certain that it is completely true.	1	2	3	4	5
25. I have struggled in trying to understand the problems of evil, suffering, and death that mark this world.	1	2	3	4	5
26. Churches should concentrate on proclaiming the gospel and not become involved in trying to change society through social or political action.	1	2	3	4	5
27. While we can never be quite sure that what we believe is absolutely true, it is worth acting on the probability that it may be.	1	2	3	4	5
28. I have found many religious questions to be difficult and complex so I am hesitant to be dogmatic or final in my assertions.	1	2	3	4	5
29. In my religion my relationships with other people are as fundamental as my relationship with God.	1	2	3	4	5
30. My religious beliefs are pretty much the same today as they were five years ago.	1	2	3	4	5

For items 31-38, please circle the number which indicates your answer.

31. If not prevented by unavoidable circumstances, I attend church:
    1. rarely or never
    2. once every month or two
    3. two or three times a month
    4. at least once a week

32. Do you hold an office or other service position in your local congregation?
    1. no   2. yes

33. How active have you been this last year in outreach or witnessing activities?
    1. rarely or never
    2. at least six times a year
    3. at least once a month
    4. at least once a week

34. Last year, approximately what percent of your gross income was contributed to the church or other religious causes?
    1. less than 5%
    2. 5% to 9%
    3. 10% to 14%
    4. 15% to 19%
    5. 20% or more

35. All in all, how important would you say your religious faith is to you?
    1. fairly unimportant
    2. not too important
    3. fairly important
    4. quite important
    5. extremely important

36. Religion always identifies a basic human problem, something that is wrong with humans and their world. Indicate the **single** most basic problem.
    1. something lacking in my individual life
    2. separation of humans from God; sinfulness
    3. lack of human community or closeness between people
    4. other_____

37. Religion always describes a path to salvation, a way that basic human problems can be overcome. Which of the following comes closest to that path?
    1. doing good works to earn God's favor
    2. trusting in God's free gift of forgiveness
    3. working hard to make society better and more just
    4. other_____

38. Finally, religion talks about the outcomes of salvation. What is the most important outcome?
    1. life on earth is changed; feel fulfillment, meaning
    2. live forever with God after the resurrection
    3. world changed so people live in peace and harmony
    4. other_____

Below are some current issues in American society. Please circle the number that shows how you feel about each one as follows: 1 = strongly oppose, 2 = somewhat oppose, 3 = uncertain, 4 = somewhat favor, 5 = strongly favor.

		strongly oppose				strongly favor
39.	United States-Soviet "freeze" on the development of nuclear weapons	1	2	3	4	5
40.	Establishment of normal, peaceful relations with Russia	1	2	3	4	5
41.	Increased government aid to improve the social and economic position of Blacks and other minorities	1	2	3	4	5
42.	Elimination of all racial restrictions in housing, education, and employment	1	2	3	4	5
43.	The Equal Rights Amendment (ERA) to the Constitution which guarantees equality to women	1	2	3	4	5
44.	Christians as individuals becoming involved in political action (run for office, work for a candidate, etc.)	1	2	3	4	5
45.	Churches as corporate entities becoming involved in political action (e.g., issuing position statements)	1	2	3	4	5
46.	A constitutional amendment to permit prayer and/or Bible reading in public schools	1	2	3	4	5
47.	Increased spending for national defense	1	2	3	4	5
48.	Military aid to the Nicaraguan "Contras"	1	2	3	4	5
49.	Government-sponsored insurance for elderly in nursing homes	1	2	3	4	5
50.	Construction of Strategic Defense Initiative (Star Wars) to ward off possible nuclear attack	1	2	3	4	5
51.	Appointment of conservative, strict-constructionist justices (such as Rehnquist, Scalia, and Bork) to the US Supreme Court	1	2	3	4	5
52.	Control of crime by tougher laws and "stiffer" sentences	1	2	3	4	5
53.	Withdrawal of the United States from the United Nations	1	2	3	4	5
54.	Registration of all firearms	1	2	3	4	5
55.	Regarding capitalism or free enterprise as that form of government most in harmony with Biblical Christianity	1	2	3	4	5
56.	Capital punishment (the death penalty) for certain classes of dangerous criminals	1	2	3	4	5

57. With which political party do you most closely identify?
   1. Democrat
   2. Republican
   3. Independent
   4. no interest in politics

58. For whom did you vote in the last presidential election?
   1. Reagan
   2. Mondale
   3. didn't vote

59. Which of the following terms best describes your political orientation?
   1. conservative
   2. moderate
   3. liberal
   4. no opinions

Please circle the answers to questions 60-63 as follows: 1=seldom or never 2=less than weekly 3=at least weekly 4=daily

		seldom or never			daily
60.	How often do you: pray privately	1	2	3	4
61.	study the Bible	1	2	3	4
62.	read religious literature	1	2	3	4
63.	participate in family worship	1	2	3	4

Please rate each of the following journals, published by Adventists but not denominationally sponsored. If not familiar with, circle NF.

		nearly worthless				very valuable
64.	OUR FIRM FOUNDATION	NF	1	2	3	4	5
65.	THE LAYWORKER	NF	1	2	3	4	5
66.	SPECTRUM	NF	1	2	3	4	5
67.	GOOD NEWS UNLIMITED	NF	1	2	3	4	5

There are many different ways of picturing God. Below are four sets of contrasting images. On a scale of 1 to 7 where would you place your picture of God in each set?

68.	MOTHER	1	2	3	4	5	6	7	FATHER
69.	MASTER	1	2	3	4	5	6	7	SPOUSE
70.	JUDGE	1	2	3	4	5	6	7	LOVER
71.	FRIEND	1	2	3	4	5	6	7	KING

Personal information:

72. Please circle the number of your sex.
    1. male 2. female

73. Circle the number that indicates the number of years you have been a baptized Adventist?
    1. less than 1 year
    2. 1 to 5 years
    3. 6 to 10 years
    4. 11 to 20 years
    5. over 20 years

74. Was at least one of your parents an Adventist sometime during the first 12 years of your life?
    1. yes
    2. no

75. What is your marital status?
    1. presently married
    2. never married
    3. separated or divorced
    4. widowed

76. Please circle the number of your age group.
    1. 19 years or less
    2. 20-35 years
    3. 36-50 years
    4. 51-65 years
    5. over 65 years

77. Please circle the number of your ethnic background.
    1. Asian   2. Black
    3. Hispanic   4. White
    5. Other

78. Please circle the number of your yearly family income:
    1. under $10,000
    2. $10,000 to $15,999
    3. $16,000 to $24,999
    4. $25,000 to $49,999
    5. $50,000 or over

79. Please circle the number of the highest level of formal education that you have completed.
    1. less than 7th grade
    2. 7th to 9th grade
    3. 10th or 11th grade
    4. high school graduation
    5. some college training
    6. four-year college degree
    7. graduate professional training (M.A., Ph.D.)

How many years have you attended Seventh-day Adventist schools on each of the following levels?

80. Elementary (grades 1-8)   _____ years
81. Secondary (grades 9-12)   _____ years
82. College or university   _____ years

PLEASE ANSWER ALL QUESTIONS!   Thank you very much!